Lincoln Christian College

P9-BZW-605

Population and the Urban Future

POPULATION AND THE URBAN FUTURE

Philip M. Hauser
Robert W. Gardner
Aprodicio A. Laquian
Salah El-Shakhs

PUBLISHED IN CO-OPERATION WITH THE
UNITED NATIONS FUND FOR POPULATION ACTIVITIES

STATE UNIVERSITY OF
NEW YORK PRESS, ALBANY

The views and opinions expressed in the various papers presented at the Conference and printed here, are not necessarily those of the United Nations Fund for Population Activities

Published by
State University of New York Press, Albany

© 1982 United Nations Fund for Population Activities

All rights reserved

Printed in the United States of America

No part of this book may be used or reproduced
in any manner whatsoever without written permission
except in the case of brief quotations embodied in
critical articles and reviews.

For information, address State University of New York
Press, State University Plaza, Albany, N.Y., 12246

Library of Congress Cataloging in Publication Data
Main entry under title:

Population and the urban future.

    1. Urbanization. 2. Population. 3. Quality of
life. 4. City planning.
HT119.P66   307.7'6   82-5529
ISBN 0-87395-591-9   AACR2
ISBN 0-87395-592-7 (pbk.)

Contents

66082

Tables

Foreword

In September 1980, the United Nations Fund for Population Activities (UNFPA) sponsored the International Conference on Population and the Urban Future in Rome, Italy. Mayors and urban planners from 41 cities which are expected to have over five million persons in the year 2000 attended the Conference; also present were national planners from the 31 countries where these cities are located.

This volume contains edited versions of the three background documents prepared for the participants of the Conference: (1) Urban Future: Trends and Prospects; (2) Issues and Instruments in Metropolitan Planning; and (3) National and Regional Instruments in Metropolitan Planning; and (3) National and Regional Issues and Policies in Facing the Challenges of the Urban Future. Also included is the Rome Declaration, adopted by the Conference by consensus. The Declaration emphasises the close interrelationship between metropolitan planning and management on the one hand, and national planning on the other. In order to meet the twin objectives of "managed population growth and planned urbanization," the Declaration calls for (1) the formulation of comprehensive national population policies by all countries by 1985; (2) policies for balanced rural-urban development; and (3) policies for improvement of urban areas.

I am glad to see that, through this volume, the background documents as well as the Declaration, which contain results of studious research and practical experience, are being made available to a wider audience. It is our belief and hope that this will contribute to a better understanding of the problems and needs of population in the urban future.

RAFAEL M. SALAS
Executive Director
United Nations Fund for
Population Activities

-1-

Urban Future: Trends and Prospects

PHILIP M. HAUSER
University of Chicago

ROBERT W. GARDNER
East-West Population Institute

Population Trends and Prospects

The urban future will in large measure determine the world future. This situation is distinctly a twentieth-century phenomenon. In prior centuries, the urban future could have had little impact on the world future because the portion of the world's peoples living in urban places was minuscule. Although it is not possible to trace world urbanization prior to the nineteenth century, it is known that by 1800 less than 3 per cent of the population of the world lived in urban places. By the end of the twentieth century, however, over half of the world's population may be inhabitants of urban areas, and the social, economic and political role of urban populations will undoubtedly dominate the world outlook.

The urban future, however, cannot be predicted with certainty. Humankind has no way of foreseeing the future except through the projection of patterns discerned in the past. Such projections cannot be regarded as predictions because the assumptions involved in projections, implicit or explicit, may not

The authors would like to acknowledge the valuable assistance of Dr Paul Wright of the East-West Population Institute in the preparation of the statistical material.

hold. Projections are useful only in indicating the possible course of events, which may not necessarily be the actual course of events. The future does not necessarily repeat the past, and one reason this statement is true is that human beings, confronted with the possible outcomes of observed trends, can intervene to change the course of events.

Although the definition of 'urban' is generally couched in demographic terms as a population agglomeration of a given minimum size, the urban place is much more than a clumping of population. As set forth below, the urban place is also a physical construct, an economic mechanism, a form of social organization, a milieu for human behaviour and a political and governmental unit. 'Urbanism as a way of life'[1] is the net effect, as evident in human behaviour, of all these facets of the urban place.

Data on total population growth by urban and rural areas are presented in some detail in the tables for the world, for the aggregates of more developed countries (MDCs) and less developed countries (LDCs) and for broad continental regions. The statistics are the product of a splicing of the two sources of data published by the United Nations.[2]

World Population Growth—Urban and Rural

Between 1920 and 1980 world population more than doubled, rising from 1,800 million to 4,374 million (Table 1.1). By 2000, according to the United Nations' projections, world population will further increase by 43 per cent to reach 6,254 million.

World urban population between 1920 and 1980 quintupled, soaring from 360 million to 1,807 million persons. Between 1980 and the century's end, urban population is projected to increase by an additional 78 per cent to reach 3,208 million.

Rural population also experienced considerable growth between 1920 and 1980, rising from 1,500 million to 2,567 million, or by 71 per cent. Moreover, rural population is projected to increase by an additional 19 per cent by 2000 to reach 3,046 million.

Between 1920 and 1980, total population in the more developed countries increased by about three-quarters (76 per cent), rising from 673 million to 1,181 million. Between 1980 and 2000 the MDCs are projected to increase by only 15 per cent to

Table 1.1 Total Population and Population by Urban and Rural Residence, 1920-2000 (in Millions)

Region	1920	1930	1940	1950†	1960	1970	1980	1990	2000
World									
Grand total	1860.0	2068.6	2295.1	2508.4	2986.0	3610.4	4374.1	5280.0	6254.4
Total urban	360.0	450.0	570.0	712.1	1012.1	1354.2	1806.8	2422.3	3208.0
Total rural	1500.0	1618.6	1725.1	1796.3	1973.9	2256.2	2567.3	2857.7	3046.4
More Developed Countries									
Total	672.7	757.9	820.6	857.5	975.8	1084.4	1181.0	1277.4	1360.2
Urban	260.0	315.0	385.0	444.4	572.7	702.9	834.4	969.2	1092.5
Rural	412.7	442.9	435.6	413.1	403.1	381.5	346.6	308.2	267.7
Less Developed Countries									
Total	1187.3	1310.7	1474.5	1650.9	2010.2	2526.4	3193.1	4002.6	4984.1
Urban	100.0	135.0	185.0	267.6	439.4	651.5	972.4	1453.1	2115.6
Rural	1087.3	1175.7	1289.5	1383.3	1570.8	1874.9	2220.7	2549.5	2868.5
Africa									
Grand total	142.9	163.8	191.5	220.2	272.8	351.7	460.9	614.1	813.7
Total urban	10.0	15.0	20.0	31.8	49.5	80.4	133.0	219.2	345.8
Total rural	132.9	148.8	171.5	188.4	223.3	271.3	327.9	394.4	467.9

†Average of 1950 figures from Population Studies No. 44 and No. 68.

Table 1.1 (Continued)

Region	1920	1930	1940	1950+	1960	1970	1980	1990	2000
Latin America									
Grand total	89.5	107.5	129.9	163.2	215.6	283.0	371.6	485.6	619.9
Total urban	20.0	30.0	40.0	66.3	106.6	162.4	240.6	343.3	466.2
Total rural	69.5	77.5	89.9	96.9	109.0	120.6	131.0	142.3	153.7
North America									
Grand total	115.7	134.2	144.3	166.1	198.7	226.4	248.8	275.1	296.2
Total urban	60.0	75.0	85.0	106.0	133.3	159.5	183.3	212.4	239.2
Total rural	55.7	59.2	59.3	60.1	65.4	66.9	65.5	62.7	57.0
Asia									
Grand total	1023.2	1120.2	1245.1	1374.0	1643.7	2028.1	2514.5	3069.8	3637.4
Total urban	90.0	115.0	160.0	216.3	341.6	482.4	689.3	992.2	1413.1
Total rural	933.3	1005.2	1085.1	1157.7	1302.1	1545.7	1825.2	2077.6	2224.3
East Asia									
Grand total	553.4	591.2	634.4	679.2	788.0	926.9	1087.7	1233.5	1370.1
Total urban	50.0	65.0	85.0	108.9	194.7	265.1	359.5	476.5	622.4
Total rural	503.4	526.2	549.4	570.3	590.3	661.8	728.2	757.0	747.7
South Asia									
Grand total	469.8	529.0	610.7	694.8	855.7	1101.2	1426.8	1836.3	2267.3
Total urban	40.0	50.0	75.0	107.4	146.9	217.3	329.8	515.7	790.7
Total rural	429.8	479.0	535.7	587.4	708.8	883.9	1097.0	1320.6	1476.6

Europe

Grand total	324.9	353.9	378.9	391.9*	425.2	459.1	486.5	513.6	539.5
Total urban	150.0	175.0	200.0	216.3	266.0	318.4	369.3	423.3	477.0
Total rural	174.9	178.9	178.9	175.6	159.2	140.7	117.2	90.3	62.5

Oceania

Grand total	8.5	10.0	11.0	12.7	15.7	19.3	23.5	28.1	32.7
Total urban	4.0	5.0	6.0	7.7	10.4	13.7	17.8	22.6	27.1
Total rural	4.5	5.0	5.0	5.0	5.3	5.6	5.7	5.5	5.6

Soviet Union

Grand total	155.3	179.0	195.0	180.1*	214.3	242.8	268.1	293.7	315.0
Total urban	25.0	35.0	60.0	70.8	104.6	137.6	173.7	209.4	239.6
Total rural	130.3	144.0	135.0	109.3	109.7	105.2	94.4	84.3	75.4

*Part of Eastern Europe transferred to the Soviet Union during and immediately following World War II.

†Average of 1950 figures from Population Studies No. 44 and No. 68.

PHILIP M. HAUSER AND ROBERT W. GARDNER

reach 1,360 million. In contrast, the LDCs between 1920 and 1980 far more than doubled, rising from 1,187 million to 3,193 million persons (an increase of 169 per cent). Moreover, they are projected to continue rapid growth to the century's end, increasing by 56 per cent in the next two decades to reach 4,984 million persons.

In the MDCs urban population more than tripled between 1920 and 1980 to reach 834 million. Moreover, urban residents are projected to increase by almost one-third between 1980 and 2000 to reach 1,093 million. In contrast, rural population in the MDCs rose between 1920 and 1930 only by 7 per cent to reach 436 million; it declined between 1920 and 1980 by 22 per cent to fall to 347 million. MDC rural population is projected to decline further in the next two decades by 23 per cent. It is for this reason, as will be seen below, that the increase in urban population in the MDCs is greater than the increase in the total population, that is, urban population growth includes more than the total population increase by reason of the shift from rural to urban residence.

In the LDCs urban population increased almost tenfold between 1920 and 1980, soaring from 100 million to 972 million. Moreover, urban residents in the LDCs are projected by the United Nations to more than double in the next two decades, to reach 2,116 million. Even while the tremendous increases in LDC urban population were occurring between 1920 and 1980, rural population, in contrast with the situation in the MDCs, more than doubled, rising from 1,087 million to 2,220 million. Rural population in the LDCs will continue relatively rapid growth, according to the United Nations, increasing by 29 per cent to reach 2,869 million in 2000.

Without question, the major factor in the differential increase of urban population in prospect to the end of this century in the MDCs and the LDCs is the difference in their projected rates of total population growth. This is evident within each of the continental regions among the MDCs and LDCs. Projected total population growth is consistently much greater in the less developed regions than in the more developed regions.

Between 1920 and 1980, European population increased by 50 per cent; and during the remainder of the century, it is projected to increase by an additional 11 per cent. Population in North

−6

America more than doubled between 1920 and 1980; but it is projected to increase by only 19 per cent during the remainder of the century. The Soviet Union increased by some 73 per cent between 1920 and 1980; but it is projected to increase by only 17 per cent during the next two decades. Although Oceania almost tripled in inhabitants between 1920 and 1980, it was, of course, a small element of total world population. It is projected to increase by an additional 39 per cent by the end of the century.

In contrast, population in Asia increased almost two-and-a-half-fold between 1920 and 1980. Furthermore, it is projected to increase by an additional 45 per cent to reach a total of 3,637 million by the century's end. At that time, it would contain 58 per cent of the total world population. South Asia tripled in population between 1920 and 1980 and is projected to increase by an additional 59 per cent in the next two decades. East Asia just about doubled its population between 1920 and 1980 and is projected to increase by 26 per cent by the end of the century. Latin America quadrupled its population between 1920 and 1980 and is projected to increase by more than two-thirds in the next two decades. Africa's population tripled between 1920 and 1980 and is projected to increase by over three-quarters by the end of the century.

With such large total population increments being in prospect in the less developed regions, it would be small wonder, indeed, if urban populations did not also burgeon.

Urban Population Growth Within the MDCs and the LDCs

There are great variations, of course, in the size and growth rates of urban populations among the MDCs and the LDCs when taken by continental region. Within the more developed regions in 1980, Europe had 369 million urban inhabitants, North America 183 million, the Soviet Union 174 million and Oceania about 18 million. By 2000 urban population in Europe, according to the United Nations' projections, would have increased by 29 per cent, in the Soviet Union by 38 per cent, in North America by 30 per cent and in Oceania by about 52 per cent.

Within the less developed regions, Asia had 689 million urban residents in 1980, with 360 million in East Asia and 330 million in

Table 1.2. Average Annual Growth Rates* for Total, Urban and Rural Populations, Each Decade 1920-2000; 1920-50; 1950-2000; and 1980-2000

Region	1920-30	1930-40	1940-50	1950-60	1960-70	1970-80	1980-90	1990-2000	1920-50	1950-2000	1980-2000
World											
Grand total	1.1	1.0	0.9	1.7	1.9	1.9	1.9	1.7	1.0	1.8	1.8
Total urban	2.2	2.4	2.2	3.5	2.9	2.9	2.9	2.8	2.3	2.5	2.9
Total rural	0.8	0.6	0.4	0.9	1.3	1.3	1.1	0.6	0.4	1.1	0.9
More Developed Countries											
Total	1.2	0.8	0.4	1.3	1.1	0.9	0.8	0.6	0.8	0.9	0.7
Urban	1.9	2.0	1.4	2.5	2.1	1.7	1.5	1.2	1.8	1.8	1.4
Rural	0.7	-0.2	-0.5	-0.3	-0.6	-1.0	-1.2	-1.4	0.0	-0.9	-1.3
Less Developed Countries											
Total	1.0	1.2	1.1	2.0	2.3	2.3	2.3	2.2	1.1	2.2	2.2
Urban	3.0	3.2	3.7	8.0	3.9	4.0	4.0	3.8	3.3	4.1	3.9
Rural	0.8	0.9	0.7	1.3	1.8	1.7	1.4	1.2	0.8	1.5	1.3
Africa											
Grand total	1.4	1.6	1.4	2.1	2.5	2.7	2.9	2.8	1.4	2.6	2.8
Total urban	4.1	2.9	4.6	4.4	4.9	5.0	5.0	4.6	3.9	4.8	4.8
Total rural	1.1	1.4	0.9	1.7	2.0	1.9	1.9	1.7	1.2	1.8	1.8
Latin America											
Grand total	1.8	1.9	2.3	2.8	2.7	2.7	2.7	2.4	2.0	2.7	2.6
Total urban	4.1	2.9	5.1	4.8	4.2	3.9	3.6	3.1	4.0	3.9	3.3
Total rural	1.1	1.5	0.8	1.2	1.0	0.8	0.8	0.8	1.1	0.9	0.8
North America											
Grand total	1.5	0.7	1.4	1.8	1.3	0.9	1.0	0.7	1.2	1.2	0.9
Total urban	2.2	1.3	2.2	2.3	1.8	1.4	1.5	1.2	1.9	1.6	1.3
Total rural	0.6	0.0	0.1	0.9	0.2	-0.2	-0.4	-1.0	0.3	-0.1	-0.7
Asia											
Grand total	0.9	1.1	1.0	1.8	2.1	2.2	2.0	0.7	1.0	2.0	1.9
Total urban	2.5	3.3	3.0	4.6	3.5	3.6	3.6	3.5	2.9	3.8	3.6
Total rural	0.7	0.8	0.7	1.2	1.7	1.7	1.3	0.7	0.7	1.3	1.0

Table 1.2. (Continued)

Region	1920-30	1930-40	1940-50	1950-60	1960-70	1970-80	1980-90	1990-2000	1920-50	1950-2000	1980-2000
East Asia											
Grand total	0.7	0.7	0.7	1.5	1.6	1.6	1.3	1.1	0.7	1.4	1.2
Total urban	2.6	2.7	2.5	5.8	3.1	3.1	2.8	2.7	2.6	3.5	2.7
Total rural	0.4	0.4	0.4	0.3	1.1	1.0	0.4	-0.1	0.4	0.5	0.1
South Asia											
Grand total	1.2	1.4	1.3	2.1	2.5	2.6	2.5	2.1	1.3	2.4	2.3
Total urban	2.2	4.1	2.7	3.1	3.9	4.2	4.5	4.3	3.3	4.0	4.4
Total rural	1.1	1.1	0.9	1.9	2.2	2.2	1.9	1.1	1.0	1.8	1.5
Europe											
Grand total	0.9	0.7	0.3*	0.8	0.8	0.6	0.5	0.5	0.6	0.6	0.5
Total urban	1.5	1.3	0.8*	2.1	1.8	1.5	1.4	1.2	1.2	1.6	1.3
Total rural	0.2	0.0	-0.2*	-1.0	1.2	-1.8	-2.6	-3.7	0.0	-2.1	-3.1
Oceania											
Grand total	1.6	1.0	1.4	2.1	2.1	2.0	1.8	1.5	1.3	1.9	1.7
Total urban	2.2	1.8	2.5	3.0	2.8	2.6	2.4	1.8	2.2	2.5	2.1
Total rural	1.1	0.0	0.0	0.6	0.6	0.2	-0.4	0.2	0.4	0.2	-0.1
Soviet Union											
Grand total	1.4	0.9	-0.8*	1.7	1.3	1.0	0.9	0.7	0.5	1.1	0.8
Total urban	3.4	5.4	1.7*	3.9	2.7	2.3	1.9	1.4	3.5	2.4	1.6
Total rural	1.0	-0.7	-2.1*	0.0	-0.4	-1.1	-1.1	-1.1	-0.6	-0.7	-1.1

*Growth rates include transfer of some territory from Eastern to the Soviet Union during the 1940-50 decade.

*Using $r = \dfrac{\ln (P_t/P_o)}{t}$ where r = growth rate, P_t and P_o are populations at time to and o, and t = length of interval.

South Asia. By 2000, Asia's urban population is projected to more than double, East Asia is to increase by 73 per cent and South Asia is to increase by 139 per cent. Latin America had 241 million urban inhabitants in 1980 and faces the prospect of a near doubling by 2000. Africa, with 133 million urban residents in 1980, is projected to experience considerably more than a doubling by 2000 (137 per cent).

Within the more developed regions in 1980, Europe had 20 per cent of the world's urban inhabitants, North America and the Soviet Union each 10 per cent and Oceania 18 per cent. By 2000, Europe is projected to have only 15 per cent of the world's urban population, the Soviet Union and North America only 7 per cent each, and Oceania less than 1 per cent.

In 1980, of the total world urban population, Asia contained 38 per cent, with 20 per cent in East Asia and 1 per cent in South Asia. In 1980, Latin America had 13 per cent of the world's total urban population and Africa 7 per cent. By 2000 Asia is projected to contain 44 per cent of the world's urban peoples, with 19 per cent in East Asia and 25 per cent in South Asia; Latin America is to have 15 per cent and Africa 11 per cent.

Average annual growth rates for total urban and rural populations for the MDCs, LDCs and continental regions are given in Table 1.2. From these data, it is clear that the LDCs are faced with severe problems in their effort to improve the levels of living of their urban populations as their urban residents double in the next two decades. Especially severe will be the problems generated in South Asia and Africa, where urban populations may more than double in the next two decades. Among the MDCs, urban population increases will be much more modest, but nevertheless not without need for significant adjustments as they experience increases of about one-third in the next two decades.

Urbanization

Urbanization refers to the proportion of a total population which inhabits urban places. In 1920 less than one-fifth (19.4 per cent) of the world's peoples lived in urban places. By 1980 urbanization had reached the level of more than two-fifths (41.3 per cent)

Table 1.3. Percentage Urban, 1920–2000

Region	1920	1930	1940	1950	1960	1970	1980	1990	2000
World	19.4	21.8	24.8	28.4	33.9	37.5	41.3	45.9	51.3
More developed countries	38.7	41.6	46.9	51.8	58.7	64.8	70.7	75.9	80.3
Less developed countries	8.4	10.3	12.6	16.2	21.9	25.8	30.5	36.3	42.5
Africa	7.0	9.2	10.4	14.4	18.2	22.9	28.9	35.7	42.5
Latin America	22.4	27.9	30.8	40.6	49.4	57.4	64.8	70.7	75.2
North American	51.9	55.9	58.9	63.8	67.1	70.5	73.7	77.2	80.8
Asia	8.8	10.3	12.9	15.7	20.8	23.8	27.4	32.3	38.9
East Asia	9.0	11.0	13.4	16.0	24.7	28.6	33.1	38.6	45.4
South Asia	8.5	9.5	12.3	15.5	17.2	19.8	23.1	28.1	34.9
Europe	46.2	49.5	52.8	55.2	62.6	69.4	75.9	82.4	88.4
Oceania	47.1	50.0	54.6	60.6	66.2	71.0	75.7	80.4	82.9
Australia–New Zealand	60.6	62.5	69.0	74.3	79.5	81.8	81.5	82.8	83.7
Soviet Union	16.1	19.6	30.8	39.3	48.8	56.7	64.8	71.3	76.1

and by 2000 is projected to exceed one-half (51.3 per cent). (Table 1.3.)

In the MDCs, 39 per cent of the population was urban in 1920, but 71 per cent was resident in urban places by 1980. By 2000, the United Nations projects that over four-fifths (80.3 per cent) of the MDC populations will be urban. In the LDCs only 8 per cent of the population was urban in 1920, but the level had reached 30 per cent in 1980. By 2000, over two-fifths (42.5 per cent) of the LDC population is projected to be living in urban places.

Variation in the levels of urbanization may, of course, be observed among both the MDCs and the LDCs by continental region. Among the MDCs, the level of urbanization by continental region in 1980 varied from 76 per cent in Europe to 65 per cent in the Soviet Union, a relatively narrow range. By the century's end, the range is projected still to be relatively narrow, falling between 82 per cent in Europe (and Oceania) to 71 per cent in the USSR. Among the MDCs, urbanization is rising to what may well be limits not too far below the 100 per cent saturation point.

Within the LDCs in 1980, Latin America was by far the most urbanized region at 65 per cent; and it is projected to reach 75 per cent urban by 2000–a level only slightly below the aggregate MDC level of 80 per cent anticipated by that date. South Asia was the least urbanized LDC region in 1980 at 22 per cent, and will remain the least urbanized by the century's end, at 35 per cent. Africa was 29 per cent urban in 1980, and will increase to 45 per cent in the next two decades. Asia, as a whole, will increase from 27 per cent urban in 1980 to 39 per cent by the end of the century.

In the world as a whole and in the MDCs as well, urban increase as a percentage of total population increase generally accelerated between 1920 and 1980 (Table 1.4). Between 1920 and 1930, urban population increase in the world accounted for 43 per cent of total population growth. Between 1970 and 1980 the figure was 59 per cent, and between 1990 and 2000 the United Nations' projections indicate that urban growth will account for over four-fifths (80.6 per cent) of total world population growth.

In the MDCs, urban areas absorbed almost two-thirds (64.6 per cent) of total population increase between 1920 and 1930. Between 1970 and 1980, urban growth actually exceeded total

Table 1.4. Urban Increase as a Percentage of Total Increase, Each Decade 1920–2000; 1920–50; 1950–2000; and 1980–2000

Region	1920–30	1930–40	1940–50	1950–60	1960–70	1970–80	1980–90	1990–2000	1920–50	1950–2000	1980–2000
World	43.1	53.0	66.6	62.8	54.8	59.3	67.9	80.6	54.3	66.6	74.5
More developed countries	64.6	111.6	161.0	108.5	119.9	136.1	139.8	148.9	99.8	128.9	144.0
Less developed countries	28.4	30.5	46.8	47.8	41.1	48.1	59.4	67.5	36.2	55.4	63.8
Africa	23.9	18.1	41.1	33.7	39.2	48.2	56.3	63.4	28.2	52.9	60.3
Latin America	55.6	44.6	79.0	76.9	82.8	88.3	90.1	91.5	62.8	87.6	90.9
North America	81.1	99.0	96.3	83.7	94.6	106.3	110.7	127.0	91.3	102.4	117.9
Asia	25.8	36.0	43.7	46.5	36.6	42.5	54.6	74.2	36.0	52.9	64.7
East Asia	39.7	46.3	53.4	78.9	50.7	58.7	80.3	107.0	46.8	74.3	93.1
South Asia	16.9	30.6	38.5	24.6	28.7	34.6	45.4	63.8	30.0	43.5	54.8
Europe	86.2	100.0	125.4	149.3	154.6	185.8	199.3	207.3	99.0	176.7	203.2
Oceania	66.7	100.0	100.0	90.0	91.7	97.6	104.4	97.8	88.1	97.0	101.1
Australia–New Zealand	71.4	142.9	107.1	100.0	92.6	80.0	90.3	90.0	100.0	90.3	90.2
Soviet Union	42.2	156.3	−72.5*	98.8	115.8	142.7	139.5	141.8	184.7	122.9	140.5

*The total national population and the rural population declined between 1940 and 1950, but the urban population increased.

population growth – the result, of course, of migration from rural to urban areas. This flow of the rural population to urban centres is expected to increase, and between 1990 and 2000 urban growth will be 149 per cent of total population increase in the MDCs.

In the LDCs, urban population growth accounted for only 28 per cent of total population growth betwen 1920 and 1930. Between 1970 and 1980, however, urban increase was almost half (48 per cent) of total population growth. During the last decade of this century, it is projected that the urban population increment in the LDCs will exceed two-thirds (68 per cent) of the total population increase.

According to the United Nations' projections, the extent to which urban growth will absorb total population growth in the more developed continental regions will vary from 90 per cent in Oceania to 203 per cent in Europe (Table 1.4). For the Soviet Union, urban growth is projected to be 140 per cent of the total population increment, and for North America 118 per cent. Thus, according to the United Nations' projections, the more developed continental regions are still faced with considerable flows of population from rural to urban areas, and therefore the need will be considerable for major accommodations in areas of both migrant origin and destination.

In none of the less developed continental regions is urban growth projected to exceed the total population increment. Urban population increase between 1980 and 2000 is projected to absorb from 25 per cent (South Asia) to 91 per cent (Latin America) of total population growth. Thus, in less developed regions, rural-to-urban population flows will be relatively small in relation to total population increase. Although the LDCs must also be prepared to deal with problems generated by internal migration both in areas of origin and in areas of destination, the more crucial problem will lie in the need to dampen rates of total population growth. This will become even more apparent as the components of urban growth are examined below.

Increases of the margin to be reported in the level of urbanization in the less developed regions point to serious exacerbation of problems which confront national, regional, and local officials, as will be discussed in Sub-section 3.2, Forces and Facets of Urbanization.

Components of Urban Growth

Population in individual urban places with fixed boundaries can grow only in two ways: by 'natural increase', the excess of births over deaths, and by 'migration and reclassification'. Reclassification includes graduation of rural places into urban places. In addition, of course, urban places may increase by extension of their boundaries. Although it is important to know the contribution of each of these components of urban growth because of their importance for policy and programmes, data in such detail are relatively scarce, especially in the LDCs. The United Nations, however, has, through its own research and the collation of the research of others, managed to obtain at least approximations of the contribution to urban growth of natural increase on the one hand, and migration and reclassification on the other.

In sample nations of the MDCs and the LDCs, based on rather complex demographic procedures, such data are being made available in a forthcoming publication.[3] For the purposes of this paper it suffices to say that the demographic statistics have been validated, and that the data are, in general, accurate enough for policy purposes.

The population experts in the United Nations used a sample of 48 nations for which data were available, some for more than one time period, to give a total of 65 observations over a period ranging from the 1950s to the 1970s. There were 40 observations for less developed countries and 25 for the more developed ones. The averages reported below, however, were based on the 'last observation only' for 29 LDCs and 20 MDCs.

In the sample of 65 observations, the United Nations has estimated that 46 per cent of urban growth was attributable to a combination of migration and reclassification, leaving 54 per cent to be the contribution of natural increase. For the MDCs, using the 20 last observations only, the annual intercensal population growth rate was 2.47 per cent. Of this growth rate, 0.97 per cent was contributed by natural increase and 1.5 per cent by migration and reclassification. Thus, for the sample of MDCs, the mean contribution of migration and reclassification to urban growth was 59.8 per cent.

Based on the last observation only for 29 LDCs, the annual

PHILIP M. HAUSER AND ROBERT W. GARDNER

intercensal growth rate was 4.32 per cent. Of this annual growth
rate, migration and reclassification contributed 1.79 per cent, and
natural increase 2.53 per cent. Thus, in the sample of LDCs,
based on the last observation only, migration and reclassification
contributed only 39.3 per cent of the annual urban growth rate, a
percentage only two-thirds of that for the MDCs. These data
support the conclusion drawn above in the discussion of the
proportion of total population increase which was absorbed by
urban areas. Natural increases are a much more important component in urban growth in the LDCs than in the MDCs—a fact
which has important implications for population policy. The conclusion is obvious: to control urban growth in the less developed
areas, it becomes much more important to control natural increase than it is in more developed areas.

There is considerable variation, of course, within the MDCs
and the LDCs in the extent to which migration and
reclassification played a role in urban growth. In accounting for
urban growth among the MDCs, migration and reclassification
ranged from 20 per cent in Australia to 94 per cent in Austria.
Among the 16 observations available for Europe, all but Norway
from 1950 to 1960 and Sweden and Switzerland had migration
and reclassification accounting for less than 50 per cent of urban
growth; and in nine countries the proportion was over 60 per
cent. The mean rate for migration and reclassification in the observations for Europe was 66.6 per cent. In the United States and
Canada, the proportion for urban growth accounted for by migration and reclassification was only 29.2 per cent and 33.7 per cent
respectively. In the U.S.S.R. migration and reclassification accounted for 61.1 per cent of urban growth; in Oceania it was 34.8
per cent.

Among the LDCs in Asia, migration and reclassification constituted less than 40 per cent of total annual growth rate in India,
Indonesia, Nepal and Syria. But migration and reclassification
constituted from 43 per cent to 63 per cent for other LDCs in
Asia: Iran, Iraq, the Republic of Korea and Turkey. In Africa,
migration and reclassification was less than 40 per cent of urban
growth in Morocco and slightly over 42 per cent in Ghana and the
Union of South Africa. In Latin America, migration and
reclassification was under 42 per cent of urban growth in El

–16

Salvador, Guatemala, Mexico, Nicaragua, Panama, Chile, Ecuador, Columbia, Paraguay, Uruguay and Venezuela. These factors accounted for over 40 per cent of urban growth, however, in Brazil and Peru, and for over 50 per cent in Argentina and Puerto Rico.

In summarizing the factors associated with net rural-to-urban migration based on much research by many scholars, the United Nations' study stresses three factors:

(i) Rising levels of personal income.

(ii) The tendency for income increases to be expended mainly on non-agricultural products.

(iii) Greater efficiency in production and consumption in urban areas.

The United Nations' study also summarized the factors which affect the rate at which urbanization occurs. Without explication here, these may be set forth as follows:

(i) More rapid technological change in agricultural than in non-agricultural activities, which accelerates movement out of rural areas.

(ii) Concentration of exports produced in the urban sector.

(iii) High natural increase in rural areas.

(iv) Institutional arrangements which limit the absorptive capacity of rural areas, such as: some land tenure systems; price and tax discriminatory policies in favour of urban populations.

(v) Biases in favour of government services for urban areas.

(vi) Inertia–a negative factor in favour of keeping population in rural areas.

(vii) Government migration policies which aim to retard rural-to-urban migration.

It is not contended that these are the only operative factors, but they lead to the conclusion that '. . . we should expect migration rates to be higher where economic growth is more rapid'. In fact the United Nations' analysis 'clearly suggests that income levels and income growth have positive effects on rates of rural out-migration'. In concluding, the United Nations' study states that the 'net flow of migrants from rural areas in developing countries seems to be fairly closely related to a country's level and rate of economic development'.

17–

PHILIP M. HAUSER AND ROBERT W. GARDNER

Urban Growth by Size of Place

Places of 20,000 and over. In an effort to achieve international comparability, the United Nations has recommended that all countries, in tabulating their census results, include tabulations for places having 20,000 or more inhabitants. Such places may be regarded, therefore, as providing a basis for a uniform international definition of urban, one to be contrasted with the country's own definitions of urban. In 1980 the population in places of 20,000 or more in the world as a whole numbered 1,374.6 million, constituting some 76 per cent of total urban population when national definitions are used. In the more developed countries, the population in places of 20,000 or more constituted 78 per cent, and in the less developed countries 75 per cent, of total urban population. The United Nations' projections indicate that there will be little change in these proportions to the end of the century (Table 1.5 a, b and c).

In the world as a whole, population in places having 20,000 or more inhabitants increased from 14 per cent of the total population in 1920 to 31 per cent in 1980. By 2000, the population in such places is projected to be 39 per cent of the world's total. In the MDCs, population in places of 20,000 and over increased from 29 per cent in 1920 to 55 per cent in 1980 and is projected to increase further to 62 per cent by the end of the century. In the LDCs, the population in such places rose from 6 per cent in 1920 to 23 per cent in 1980 and is projected to rise to just short of one-third of the total population by 2000 (32 per cent). The variations in percentage of total population in places of 20,000 or more within the MDCs in 1980 ranged from 48 per cent in the Soviet Union to 61 per cent in North America. Europe had 58 per cent of its population in such places and Oceania 52 per cent. By the end of the century the Soviet Union will still have the smallest proportion of population in places of 20,000 and over, at 56 per cent. Oceania will have increased its proportion to 76 per cent, Europe to 68 per cent and North America to 66 per cent.

Within the less developed continental regions, population in places of 20,000 or more in 1980 ranged from 21 per cent in Africa to 43 per cent in Latin America. Asia had 22 per cent of its population living in such places, averaging 27 per cent in East

Table 1.5. Three Characteristics of Population in Cities of Size 20,000 +, 1920–2000

(a) Total Population (in Millions)

Region	1920	1930	1940	1950	1960	1970	1980	1990	2000
World	266.4	338.2	431.5	542.2	777.3	1028.6	1374.6	1835.5	2426.0
More developed countries	197.7	247.1	303.9	350.1	443.9	548.1	648.9	751.3	847.3
Less developed countries	68.7	91.1	127.6	192.1	333.4	480.5	725.7	1084.2	1578.7
Africa	6.9	9.7	13.8	22.1	36.1	57.3	95.5	158.9	251.5
Latin America	12.9	18.1	25.5	41.5	70.8	108.7	160.4	227.8	312.6
North America	47.9	62.4	66.6	84.7	109.8	129.7	150.9	178.0	195.4
Asia	66.7	88.4	124.3	172.0	270.5	376.5	544.1	776.1	1105.4
East Asia	39.8	53.9	73.7	97.6	159.1	213.5	295.0	388.3	507.3
South Asia	26.9	34.5	50.6	75.3	111.4	163.1	249.4	386.7	598.1
Europe	112.9	131.8	149.8	164.3	204.0	242.8	282.7	322.1	368.0
Oceania	3.1	3.8	4.5	6.1	8.6	10.7	12.3	18.0	20.5
Soviet Union	16.0	24.0	47.0	50.6	77.7	103.1	128.7	154.4	177.0

Table 1.5. (Continued)

(b) As Percentage of Urban Population

Region	1920	1930	1940	1950	1960	1970	1980	1990	2000
World	74.0	75.2	75.7	76.1	76.8	76.0	76.1	75.8	75.6
More developed countries	76.0	78.4	78.9	78.8	77.5	78.0	77.8	77.5	77.6
Less developed countries	68.7	67.5	69.0	71.8	75.9	73.8	74.6	74.6	74.6
Africa	63.0	64.7	69.0	69.5	72.9	71.3	71.8	72.5	72.7
Latin America	64.5	60.3	63.8	62.6	66.4	66.9	66.7	66.4	67.1
North America	79.8	83.2	78.4	79.9	82.4	81.3	82.3	83.8	81.7
Asia	74.1	76.9	77.7	79.9	79.2	78.1	78.9	78.8	78.2
East Asia	79.6	82.9	86.7	89.6	81.7	80.5	82.1	81.5	81.5
South Asia	67.3	69.0	67.5	70.1	75.8	75.1	75.6	75.0	75.6
Europe	75.3	75.3	74.9	76.0	76.7	76.3	76.6	76.1	77.2
Oceania	77.5	76.0	75.0	79.2	82.7	78.1	69.1	79.7	76.4
Soviet Union	64.0	68.6	78.3	71.5	74.3	74.9	74.1	73.7	73.9

(c) *As Percentage of Total Population*

Region	1920	1930	1940	1950	1960	1970	1980	1990	2000
World	14.3	16.4	18.8	21.6	26.0	28.5	31.4	34.8	38.8
More developed countries	29.4	32.6	37.0	40.8	45.5	50.5	54.9	58.8	62.3
Less developed countries	5.8	7.0	8.7	11.6	16.6	19.0	22.7	27.1	31.7
Africa	4.4	5.9	7.2	10.0	13.2	16.3	20.7	25.9	30.9
Latin America	14.4	16.8	19.6	25.4	32.8	38.4	43.2	46.9	50.4
North America	41.4	46.5	46.2	51.0	55.3	57.3	60.7	64.7	66.0
Asia	6.5	7.9	10.0	12.6	16.5	18.6	21.6	25.3	30.4
East Asia	7.2	9.1	11.6	14.4	20.2	23.0	27.1	31.5	37.0
South Asia	5.7	6.5	8.3	10.8	13.0	14.9	17.5	21.1	26.4
Europe	34.8	37.2	39.5	41.9	48.0	52.9	58.1	62.7	68.2
Oceania	36.5	38.0	40.9	48.0	54.8	55.4	52.3	64.1	75.6
Soviet Union	10.3	13.4	24.1	28.1	36.3	42.5	48.0	52.6	56.2

Asia and 17 per cent in South Asia. By the end of the century Africa will still have the lowest proportion of population in such places, at 31 per cent; and Latin America will have the largest proportion, at 50 per cent. Asia in 2000 will have 30 per cent of its people in places of 20,000 and over: East Asia 37 per cent and South Asia 26 per cent.

In general, the pattern in the proportion of population in places of 20,000 and over parallels that already given for urban population based on each nation's own definition of urban.

Places of 100,000 and over. The population distribution in places of 100,000 or more is of special importance. At this size, there can be little disagreement about the population clumping having 'urban' characteristics and being subjected to the impact of 'urbanism as a way of life'. In the world as a whole, between 1920 and 1980, the population in cities of 100,000 or more increased almost sevenfold to reach a total of 1,178 million inhabitants (Table 1.6). The United Nations' projections to the end of the century indicate that population in such cities will almost double in the next two decades.

In the more developed countries, population in cities of 100,000 or more quadrupled between 1920 and 1980 and is projected to increase by over a third (35 per cent) in the next two decades. Rapid as has been the growth of population in such cities in the MDCs, growth has been even more explosive in the LDCs. Between 1920 and 1980, population in cities of 100,000 or more increased nineteenfold, and is projected to increase by almost two-and-one-half fold by the end of the century.

In the world as a whole, population resident in cities of 100,000 and over rose from 9 per cent in 1920 to 27 per cent in 1980 and is projected to increase to 36 per cent by the end of the century (Table 3.6a). In the MDCs, inhabitants of such large cities rose from 20 per cent in 1920 to 47 per cent in 1980 and they are projected to constitute 55 per cent of total population by 2000. In the LDCs, population in such large-sized cities increased from less than 3 per cent of the total population in 1920 to 20 per cent in 1980, and is projected to increase to 20 per cent in the next two decades.

Variations in the population increases of cities of this size in

Table 1.6 Three Characteristics of Population in Cities of Size 100.000+, 1920–2000

(a) *Total Population* (in Millions)

Region	1920	1930	1940	1950	1960	1970	1980	1990	2000
World	169.8	223.3	288.8	385.4	597.2	833.1	1177.6	1627.8	2245.7
More developed countries	137.6	177.3	217.7	252.7	360.7	461.6	554.1	665.6	750.4
Less developed countries	32.2	46.0	71.1	132.7	236.5	371.4	623.5	962.2	1495.3
Africa	3.1	5.0	7.6	14.0	26.9	46.4	86.2	141.2	249.1
Latin America	8.5	12.1	18.0	30.7	56.1	96.5	157.8	237.8	354.9
North America	39.4	52.9	55.9	72.4	107.8	139.6	150.0	179.1	197.3
Asia	34.2	48.1	74.0	113.2	182.9	269.8	434.6	653.0	970.1
East Asia	21.2	31.2	46.4	64.2	106.5	146.9	229.8	319.4	431.2
South Asia	13.0	16.9	27.7	49.0	76.4	122.9	204.8	333.6	538.9
Europe	74.0	87.9	99.9	118.7	161.5	193.7	232.1	271.9	308.2
Oceania	2.6	3.3	4.0	5.0	7.0	9.3	12.4	15.9	18.4
Soviet Union	8.0	14.0	30.0	31.5	55.0	77.7	104.5	129.7	147.7

Table 1.6. (Continued)

(b) As Percentage of Urban Population

Region	1920	1930	1940	1950	1960	1970	1980	1990	2000
World	47.2	49.6	50.6	54.1	59.0	61.5	65.2	67.2	70.0
More developed countries	52.9	56.3	56.6	65.7	63.0	65.7	66.4	68.7	68.9
Less developed countries	32.3	34.1	38.4	49.6	52.8	57.0	64.1	66.2	70.7
Africa	31.0	33.3	38.0	44.0	54.3	57.7	64.8	64.4	72.0
Latin America	42.5	40.3	45.0	46.3	52.6	59.4	65.6	69.3	76.1
North America	65.7	70.5	65.8	68.3	80.9	87.5	81.8	84.3	82.5
Asia	38.0	41.8	46.3	52.3	53.5	55.9	63.1	65.8	68.7
East Asia	42.4	48.0	52.6	59.0	54.7	55.4	63.9	67.0	69.3
South Asia	32.5	33.8	36.9	44.7	52.0	56.6	62.1	64.7	68.2
Europe	49.3	50.2	50.0	54.9	60.7	60.8	62.9	64.2	64.6
Oceania	65.0	66.0	66.7	64.9	67.3	68.8	69.7	70.4	67.9
Soviet Union	32.0	40.0	50.0	44.5	52.6	56.5	60.1	61.9	61.6

(c) *As Percentage of Total Population*

Region	1920	1930	1940	1950	1960	1970	1980	1990	2000
World	9.1	10.8	12.6	15.4	20.0	23.1	26.9	30.8	35.9
More developed countries	20.5	23.4	26.5	29.5	37.0	42.6	46.9	52.1	55.2
Less developed countries	2.7	3.5	4.8	8.0	11.8	14.7	19.5	24.0	30.0
Africa	2.2	3.1	4.0	6.4	9.9	13.2	18.7	23.0	30.6
Latin America	9.6	11.3	13.9	18.8	26.0	34.1	42.5	49.0	57.3
North America	34.7	39.4	38.7	43.6	54.3	61.7	60.5	65.1	66.6
Asia	3.3	4.3	6.0	8.2	11.1	13.3	17.3	21.3	26.7
East Asia	3.8	5.3	7.3	9.5	13.5	15.9	21.1	25.9	31.5
South Asia	2.8	3.2	4.5	7.1	8.9	11.2	14.4	18.2	23.8
Europe	22.8	24.8	26.4	30.3	38.0	42.2	47.7	52.9	57.1
Oceania	30.6	33.0	36.4	39.4	44.6	48.2	52.8	56.6	56.3
Soviet Union	5.2	7.8	15.4	17.5	25.7	32.0	39.0	44.2	46.9

the continental regions of the MDCs and the LDCs respectively may be observed in their net effect, that is, in the extent to which they constitute proportions of the total population in these regions. In Europe, population in cities of 100,000 or more rose from 23 per cent of the total population in 1920 to 48 per cent in 1980 and is projected to rise further, to 57 per cent, by 2000. In North America population in such cities rose from 35 per cent in 1920 to 60 per cent in 1980, and is projected to increase further, to 67 per cent, by 2000. In the USSR such city residents made up only 5 per cent of the total population in 1920; they are 39 per cent in 1980, and are projected to increase to 47 per cent in the next two decades. In Oceania, population in cities of 100,000 or more increased from 31 percent in 1920 to 54 per cent in 1980 and will rise further, to 56 per cent, by the year 2000.

Despite the much more rapid, large-city growth in the LDCs, such large-scale city dwellers will still constitute relatively small proportions of the total population. In Asia, the population in such cities made up only 3 per cent of the total population in 1920, but rose to 17 per cent by 1980 and is projected to increase to 27 per cent by 2000. In East Asia the comparable figures are 4 per cent, 21 per cent and 31 percent; and in South Asia 3 per cent, 15 per cent and 24 per cent. In Africa, the population in cities of 100,000 and more was a little over 2 per cent in 1920, rose to 19 per cent in 1980 and is scheduled to reach 31 per cent by 2000. In Latin America, the most urbanized of the less developed regions, the proportion of total population resident in cities of 100,000 or more was about 10 per cent in 1920, reached 42 per cent by 1980, and is projected to increase to 57 percent by the end of the century.

It is apparent that, although populations in places of 20,000 and more in the LDCs will soar during the remainder of this century, relatively small proportions of their total populations compared with the MDCs will be resident in the larger cities in which, it may be anticipated, urban problems will be much more severe than in the smaller places. However, given the serious deficiency in urban amenities in the LDCs and the social, economic and political problems which already exist, there can be little doubt that the relatively rapid large-scale increases which still face the LDCs will exacerbate their already difficult problems.

Table 1.7. Three Characteristics of Population in Cities of Size 1,000,000 + , 1920–2000

(a) Total Population (in Millions)

Region	1920	1930	1940	1950	1960	1970	1980	1990	2000
World	67.7	98.7	129.1	174.5	294.6	433.1	653.0	983.7	1366.7
More developed countries	60.8	86.0	108.4	124.3	181.2	239.2	313.6	388.5	434.8
Less developed countries	6.9	12.7	20.7	50.2	113.4	193.9	339.4	595.1	931.8
Africa	0.0	1.1	1.5	3.5	7.5	15.4	36.5	83.4	154.6
Latin America	3.6	5.6	7.1	15.3	31.0	56.4	101.3	164.2	232.2
North America	18.4	29.9	31.7	40.7	63.5	88.1	114.5	144.4	159.1
Asia	11.7	17.5	30.0	49.0	95.4	149.4	237.8	390.4	589.7
East Asia	7.6	14.1	22.9	31.1	62.1	90.5	131.9	191.3	261.5
South Asia	4.1	3.4	7.1	17.9	33.3	58.9	105.9	199.1	328.2
Europe	34.0	38.7	47.6	55.1	80.3	97.8	117.1	136.3	155.4
Oceania	0.0	1.2	2.4	3.1	4.0	5.0	7.2	11.9	13.4
Soviet Union	0.0	4.7	8.6	7.9	13.0	21.1	38.6	53.0	62.3

Table 1.7. (Continued)

(b) As Percentage of Urban Population

Region	1920	1930	1940	1950	1960	1970	1980	1990	2000
World	18.8	21.9	22.7	24.5	29.1	32.0	36.1	40.6	42.6
More developed countries	23.4	27.3	28.2	28.0	31.6	33.8	37.6	40.1	39.8
Less developed countries	6.9	9.4	11.2	18.8	25.8	29.8	34.9	40.9	44.0
Africa	0.0	7.3	7.5	11.0	15.2	19.2	27.4	38.1	44.7
Latin America	18.0	16.8	17.8	23.1	29.1	34.7	42.1	47.8	49.8
North America	30.7	39.9	37.3	38.4	47.6	55.2	62.5	68.0	66.5
Asia	13.0	15.2	18.8	22.7	27.9	43.7	34.5	39.4	41.7
East Asia	15.2	21.7	26.9	28.6	31.9	34.1	36.7	40.2	42.0
South Asia	10.3	6.8	9.5	16.7	22.7	27.1	32.1	38.6	41.5
Europe	22.7	22.1	23.8	25.5	30.2	30.7	31.7	32.2	32.6
Oceania	0.0	24.0	40.0	40.3	38.5	36.5	40.5	52.7	49.5
Soviet Union	0.0	13.4	14.3	11.2	12.4	15.3	22.2	25.3	26.0

(c) *As Percentage of Total Population*

Region	1920	1930	1940	1950	1960	1970	1980	1990	2000
World	3.6	4.8	5.6	7.0	9.9	12.0	14.9	18.6	21.9
More developed countries	9.0	11.4	13.2	14.5	18.6	22.1	26.6	30.4	32.0
Less developed countries	0.6	1.0	1.4	3.0	5.6	7.7	10.6	14.9	18.7
Africa	0.0	0.7	0.8	1.6	2.8	4.4	7.9	13.6	19.0
Latin America	4.0	5.2	5.5	9.7	14.4	19.9	27.3	33.8	37.5
North America	15.9	22.3	22.0	24.9	32.0	38.9	46.0	52.5	53.7
Asia	1.1	1.6	2.4	3.6	5.8	7.4	9.5	12.7	16.2
East Asia	1.4	2.4	3.6	4.6	7.9	9.8	12.1	15.5	19.1
South Asia	0.9	0.6	1.2	2.6	3.9	5.4	7.4	10.8	14.5
Europe	10.5	10.9	12.6	14.1	18.9	21.3	24.1	26.5	28.8
Oceania	0.0	12.0	21.8	24.4	25.5	25.9	30.6	42.4	41.0
Soviet Union	0.0	2.6	4.4	4.4	6.1	8.7	14.4	18.1	19.8

PHILIP M. HAUSER AND ROBERT W. GARDNER

Places of 1,000,000 and over. There is some doubt whether cities of a million or more existed prior to the beginning of the nineteenth century. If they did, the facts cannot be documented, but reasonably sound data are available on cities of this size for the world as a whole since 1800. It is well to bear in mind that cities of a million or more could not be achieved by humankind until after considerable development of both technology and social organization.

By 1920, the population in cities of one million or more was just short of 68 million (Table 1.7). In 1980 the population in such great cities has increased almost tenfold to reach 653 million. Population in cities of this size is still increasingly rapidly so that by 2000, according to United Nations' projections, it will more than double, to reach 1,367 million.

In the MDCs, population in cities of a million or more quintupled between 1920 and 1980 and is projected to increase by almost two-fifths (39 per cent) by the end of the century. The LDC population in cities of one million or more soared almost fifty-fold between 1920 and 1980 and is projected nearly to triple in the next two decades.

Data are available from the United Nations on the number of cities of one million or more persons from 1950 and projected to 2000. For the world as a whole, cities of this size will increase from 235 in 1980 to 439 in 2000, an increase of 54 per cent. In the MDCs, there were 117 cities of this size in 1980; it is projected that this number will increase to 155 by the end of the century. In the LDCs, there were 118 cities of this size in 1980, while it is projected that there will be 284 by 2000. Thus the LDCs had 50 per cent of the world's total great cities in 1980, but they are projected to have 65 per cent by the end of the century.

Places of 5,000,000 and over. This Conference focuses on cities of 5 million or more persons. In 1920 the total population in the world living in such super-cities numbered about 15.2 million, all residents in the MDCs (Table 1.8). By 1980, population in these cities totalled 260 million, a seventeenfold increase, with an almost equal distribution between the MDCs and the LDCs. There were about 131 million people in such supercities in the MDCs and 129 million in the LDCs.

– 30

Table 1.8. Three Characteristics of Population in Cities of Size 5,000,000 + , 1920–2000

(a) Total Population (in Millions)

Region	1920	1930	1940	1950	1960	1970	1980	1990	2000
World	15.2	30.4	33.9	52.9	103.6	172.4	252.3	398.3	658.1
More developed countries	15.2	30.4	33.9	47.1	78.6	99.2	120.4	148.6	171.6
Less developed countries	0.0	0.0	0.0	5.8	24.0	73.2	131.8	249.7	486.5
Africa	0.0	0.0	0.0	0.0	0.0	5.5	7.5	15.7	58.3
Latin America	0.0	0.0	0.0	5.2	12.0	32.6	50.6	85.1	147.5
North America	8.0	10.3	10.9	12.3	29.0	35.5	45.6	59.2	71.6
Asia	0.0	6.1	8.6	12.5	29.4	57.5	103.3	183.7	315.9
East Asia	0.0	6.1	8.6	12.5	23.9	44.8	58.1	85.2	125.2
South Asia	0.0	0.0	0.0	0.0	5.5	12.9	45.2	98.4	190.7
Europe	7.2	14.0	14.4	22.7	26.9	33.1	37.6	46.0	50.4
Oceania	0.0	0.0	0.0	0.0	0.0	0.0	0.0	0.0	0.0
Soviet Union	0.0	0.0	0.0	0.0	6.3	7.1	7.7	8.5	14.4

Table 1.8. (Continued)

(b) As Percentage of Urban Population

Region	1920	1930	1940	1950	1960	1970	1980	1990	2000
World	4.2	6.8	6.0	6.6	10.2	12.7	14.0	16.4	20.5
More developed countries	5.9	9.7	8.8	10.6	13.7	14.1	14.4	15.3	15.7
Less developed countries	0.0	0.0	0.0	2.2	5.5	10.4	13.6	17.2	23.0
Africa	0.0	0.0	0.0	0.0	0.0	6.8	5.6	7.2	16.9
Latin America	0.0	0.0	0.0	7.8	11.3	20.1	21.0	24.8	31.6
North America	13.3	12.1	12.8	11.6	22.1	22.3	24.9	27.9	29.9
Asia	0.0	6.8	5.4	5.8	8.6	11.9	15.0	18.4	22.4
East Asia	0.0	9.4	10.1	11.5	12.3	16.9	16.2	17.9	20.1
South Asia	0.0	0.0	0.0	0.0	5.1	5.9	13.7	16.5	15.8
Europe	4.8	8.0	7.2	10.5	10.1	10.4	10.2	10.9	10.6
Oceania	0.0	0.0	0.0	0.0	0.0	0.0	0.0	0.0	0.0
Soviet Union	0.0	0.0	0.0	0.0	6.0	5.2	4.4	4.1	6.0

(c) *As Percentage of Total Population*

Region	1920	1930	1940	1950	1960	1970	1980	1990	2000
World	0.8	1.5	1.5	2.1	3.5	4.8	5.8	7.5	10.5
More developed countries	2.3	4.0	4.1	4.1	8.1	9.2	10.2	11.6	12.6
Less developed countries	0.0	0.0	0.0	0.4	1.2	2.9	4.1	6.4	9.8
Africa	0.0	0.0	0.0	0.0	0.0	1.6	1.6	2.6	7.2
Latin America	0.0	0.0	0.0	3.2	5.6	11.5	13.6	17.5	23.8
North America	6.9	7.7	7.6	7.4	14.6	15.7	18.3	21.5	24.2
Asia	0.0	0.5	0.7	0.9	1.5	2.8	4.1	6.0	8.7
East Asia	0.0	1.0	1.4	1.8	3.0	4.8	5.3	6.9	9.1
South Asia	0.0	0.0	0.0	0.0	0.6	1.2	3.2	5.4	8.4
Europe	2.2	4.0	3.8	5.8	6.3	7.4	7.7	9.0	9.3
Oceania	0.0	0.0	0.0	0.0	0.0	0.0	0.0	0.0	0.0
Soviet Union	0.0	0.0	0.0	0.0	2.9	3.9	2.9	2.9	4.6

By 2000 the number of people resident in cities of 5 million and more in the world is projected by the United Nations to reach 658 million: 172 million in the MDCs and 486 million in the LDCs. Thus by 2000 such super-city populations will have increased 150 per cent since 1980, by about one-third (34 per cent) in the MDCs and by about 300 per cent in the LDCs.

It is instructive to see the change in such super-city populations as a percentage of the total population. In 1920 the population in such cities constituted less than one per cent of the total world population and only 2.3 per cent of the MDC population (Table 1.8). (There were no such cities in the LDCs at that time). In 1980 such super-city inhabitants made up about 6 per cent of the total world population, 10 per cent of the MDC population and only 4 per cent of the total LDC population. The United Nations' projections show that by 2000 cities of this size could contain about 11 per cent of the total world population, 13 per cent of the MDC population and about 10 per cent of the LDC population.

The proportion of all urban residents who inhabit cities of 5 million or more is also of interest. In 1920 about 4 per cent of the world urban population was in cities of such size, and about 6 per cent of the MDC urban population. In 1980 inhabitants of such cities constituted 13.9 per cent of the world urban population, 14.4 per cent of MDC urban population and 13.6 per cent of the urban population of the LDCs. By the year 2000, according to the United Nations, about 21 per cent of the total world urban residents will live in such super-cities: 16 per cent of the MDC urban population and 23 per cent of the LDC urban population. (The population in super-cities of 5 million or more is shown by continental region in both the MDCs and LDCs in Table 1.8c. The differential growth rates of population in such cities are most succinctly considered in relation to the total regional populations.)

Within the more developed continental regions, North America in 1980 had 18 per cent of its total population in cities of 5 million or more inhabitants. This proportion is projected by the United Nations to increase to 24 per cent by 2000. Europe had almost 8 per cent of its total population in such super-cities in 1980, and is projected to increase this proportion to over 9 per cent by 2000. The Soviet Union had less than 3 per cent of its population in such cities in 1980 and is projected to increase its proportion to less than 5 per cent by 2000. Oceania has no such super-cities and is projected still to have none by the end of the century.

Among the less developed regions, Asia had only 4 per cent of its population in cities of 5 million or more, with 5 per cent in East Asia and 3 per cent in South Asia. Latin America had 14 per cent of its population in such cities in 1980 and is projected to increase this proportion to about 24 per cent by the end of the century. Africa had less than 2 per cent of its population in such places in 1980 and is projected to increase this proportion to a little over 7 per cent in the next two decades.

World's 30 largest cities. The United Nations has also traced the growth of the 30 largest cities from 1950 to 2000 (Table 1.9). Again, one must caution that problems arising from differences in boundaries require care in interpretation. The data presented here are consistent with the trends in city growth reported above.

In 1950, 11 of the largest 15 cities in the world were in the MDCs. By 1975 only eight of the 15 were in the MDCs, and by 2000 only three will still be in the MDCs: Tokyo, New York and Los Angeles. In 1950, there were only two urban areas with more than 10 million inhabitants: the New York–North-eastern New Jersey complex and London. By 1975, there were seven such areas. The five new ones included Tokyo–Yokohama, Mexico City, Shanghai, Los Angeles–Long Beach and Sao Paulo. By 2000, there will be 25 such urban areas, with five having populations projected to be in excess of 20 million: Mexico City (31.0 million), Sao Paulo (25.8 million), Tokyo–Yokohama (24.2 million), New York–North-eastern New Jersey (22.8 million), and Shanghai (22.7 million). Needless to say, these projections are not to be taken as predictions, because various types of limits may become operative in the years ahead. There is evidence that long before such fantastically large cities emerge, there is a point at which diseconomies, disamenities and dissocialities may preclude such continued growth.

Furthermore, it is to be observed that there is increasing indication that large cities since 1975 are either failing to increase or are actually losing population. Of 18 countries studied recently,

Table 1.9. The World's 30 Largest Agglomerations, Ranked by Size, and Population in Millions, 1950–2000

Rank	1950		1975		1990		2000	
1.	New York–NE New Jersey	12.3	New York–NE New Jersey	19.8	Tokyo–Yokohama	23.4	Mexico City	31.0
2.	London	10.4	Tokyo–Yokohama	17.7	Mexico City	22.9	São Paulo	25.8
3.	Rhein–Ruhr	6.9	Mexico City	11.9	New York–NE New Jersey	21.8	Tokyo–Yokohama	24.2
4.	Tokyo–Yokohama	6.7	Shanghai	11.6	São Paulo	19.9	New York–NE New Jersey	22.8
5.	Shanghai	5.8	Los Angeles–Long Beach	10.8	Shanghai	17.7	Shanghai	22.7
6.	Paris	5.5	São Paulo	10.7	Beijing	15.3	Beijing	19.9
7.	Buenos Aires	5.3	London	10.4	Rio de Janeiro	14.7	Rio de Janeiro	19.0
8.	Chicago–NW Indiana	4.9	Buenos Aires	9.3	Los Angeles–Long Beach	13.3	Greater Bombay	17.1
9.	Moscow	4.8	Rhein–Ruhr	9.3	Greater Bombay	12.0	Calcutta	16.7
10.	Calcutta	4.4	Paris	9.2	Calcutta	11.9	Jakarta	16.6
11.	Los Angeles–Long Beach	4.0	Rio de Janeiro	8.9	Seoul	11.8	Seoul	14.2
12.	Osaka–Kobe	3.8	Beijing	8.7	Buenos Aires	11.4	Los Angeles–Long Beach	14.2
13.	Milan	3.6	Osaka–Kobe	8.6	Jakarta	11.4	Cairo–Gaza–Imbaba	13.1
14.	Mexico City	3.0	Chicago–NW Indiana	8.1	Paris	10.9	Madras	12.9
15.	Philadelphia–New Jersey	2.9	Calcutta	7.8	Osaka–Kobe	10.7	Manila	12.3
16.	Rio de Janeiro	2.9	Moscow	7.4	Cairo–Gaza–Imbaba	10.0	Buenos Aires	12.1
17.	Greater Bombay	2.9	Greater Bombay	7.0	London	10.0	Bangkok–Thonburi	11.9
18.	Detroit	2.8	Seoul	6.8	Rhein–Ruhr	9.3	Karachi	11.8
19.	Naples	2.8	Cairo–Gaza–Imbaba	6.4	Bogotá	8.9	Delhi	11.7
20.	Leningrad	2.6	Milan	6.1	Chicago–NW Indiana	8.9	Bogotá	11.7
21.	Manchester	2.5	Jakarta	5.7	Madras	8.8	Paris	11.3
22.	Birmingham	2.5	Philadelphia–New Jersey	4.8	Manila	8.6	Teheran	11.3
23.	São Paulo	2.5	Detroit	4.8	Moscow	8.5	Istanbul	11.2
24.	Cairo–Gaza–Imbaba	2.5	Manila	4.5	Teheran	8.3	Baghdad	11.1
25.	Tienjin	2.4	Delhi	4.4	Istanbul	8.3	Osaka–Kobe	11.1
26.	Boston	2.2	Tienjin	4.4	Baghdad	8.2	London	9.9
27.	Shenyang	2.2	Teheran	4.3	Delhi	8.1	Dacca	9.7
28.	Beijing	2.2	Leningrad	4.2	Karachi	7.9	Chicago–NW Indiana	9.4
29.	West Berlin	2.2	Madras	4.1	Bangkok–Thonburi	7.5	Rhein–Ruhr	9.2
30.	San Francisco–Oakland	2.0	Bogotá	4.0	Milan	7.4	Moscow	9.1

SOURCE: United Nations, Population Studies No. 68, Table 4.7.

11 showed either reversal in the direction of net population flow from sparsely-settled parts of the nations in which they were located to the densely-populated core, or a drastic reduction in the level of the net flow.[4] A similar pattern is observable in the United States, in which, between 1970 and 1975, non-metropolitan counties grew more rapidly than the metropolitan ones.[5]

As the United Nations points out, the projection of city growth, even to the end of this century, indicates that 'the world is entering uncharted territory'.[6] The projections show that, by 2000, 14 cities in the world could be larger than any that existed in 1950. The smallest of the 30 largest cities as projected to 2000 would have a population of 9.1 million; and the cities which are the focus of this Conference, those with at least 5 million inhabitants, would number some 60 by the turn of the century (Table 1.1).

With this brief overview of trends in urban growth and urbanization concluded, what follows is a consideration of the antecedents and consequences of urban growth and urbanization in the world and in the MDCs and LDCs.

Forces and Facets of Urbanization

Antecedents of Urbanization in the MDCs and the LDCs

In the MDCs urbanization was both an antecedent and a consequence of increased productivity and higher levels of living. As population agglomeration occurred it was accompanied by greater division of labour, increased specialization, easier application of non-human energy, acceleration of the scientific and technological revolutions, and increasing economies of scale. Furthermore, increased size and density of population led to minimization of the frictions of time and space and the gains of external economies. In the MDCs urbanization has been a continuous and an apparently irreversible process. Although there are some similarities in the urbanization processes of the MDCs and LDCs, there are also important differences. In the urbanization of the MDCs and LDCs respectively, important disparities existed and still exist in:

(i) The forces which generate urbanization.
(ii) The ratios of population to resources and to levels of living.
(iii) The basic outlooks and values, and
(iv) The world political situation.

Forces of Urbanization

There are a number of forces that were operative during the urbanization of the MDCs which have applied differently in the less developed countries. These include the impact of the colonial heritage of the LDCs; the greater importance of total population growth rates in rapid urban growth and urbanization; the availability of twentieth-century technology to the LDCs as they experienced their economic and urban 'takeoffs'; and the greater role of central planning.

Colonial heritage. In the less developed countries, early urban growth was not so much the product of indigenous economic development as the product of colonialism, which led to the emergence of the 'primate' or 'great' city as an *entrepôt* between the colony and the mother imperial country. Primate cities tend to be many times the size of the second city and contain a much larger proportion of the total urban population than has usually been the case in the MDCs. With the disruption of empire after World War II, followed by the breaking off of economic as well as political relationships between mother country and colony, many of the primate cities in the LDCs lost a major part of the economic function which led to their growth. Where this has occurred, further indigenous economic growth is required to justify the size of the primate city. In general, the LDCs have much larger urban populations than is warranted by their degree of industrialization, using as a standard the relationship between city size and industrialization as experienced in the MDCs. This has led to characterizing the LDCs as 'over-urbanized'. Such characterization is not intended in a normative sense but rather merely to point to the difference between the MDCs and LDCs in the degree of industrialization that accompanied urban growth.

A considerable part of the acceleration in the growth of cities in the LDCs since the end of World War II may also be regarded, at least in part, as a result of their colonial heritage. Disorganization created by the war itself led to large movements of rural population to urban places for purposes of security. Moreover, with the disappearance of imperialistic control of the less developed countries, such national unity as was imposed by imperial force tended to disintegrate. This led to internal conflicts, often violent, between varying ethnic, religious, cultural or territorial groups. The insecurity engendered by such conflict also produced large streams of refugees from rural to urban places.

Total population growth. As has been indicated above in another context, the role of total population growth has been more important in accounting for urban growth in the LDCs than it was in the MDCs. In the MDCs, much larger proportions of urban growth were attributable to internal migration–flows of population from rural to urban areas. Cityward flows of population in the MDCs were much more generated by the pull of higher wages resulting from increased productivity in the urban setting. In contrast, it appears that internal migratory flows to urban places in the LDCs have more often been generated by push rather than pull factors. In any case natural increase, the excess of birth over deaths, is more prominent in accounting for urban growth in the LDCs than it was in the MDCs.

Twentieth-century technology. Another significant factor accounting for differences in urbanization in the LDCs and MDCs is to be found in the availability of twentieth-century technology as urbanization accelerates in the former. The availability of twentieth-century technology may have an impact on LDC urbanization in at least two ways: first, in affecting the rate of urban growth, especially as rural-to-urban migration is concerned; and second, as it may affect spatial patterns within the urban area.

The adoption of twentieth-century technology in efforts to achieve development may lead to capital-intensive rather than to

39–

labour-intensive industrialization. Such a course in respect to agriculture tends to push agricultural labour cityward; and, in respect to industrial growth, it limits the capacity of the urban area for labour absorption. Thus rural-to-urban migration may be accelerated even while job opportunities in the city are limited.

The availability of twentieth-century technology may also affect spatial patterns within LDC urban areas. In the MDCs, the spatial pattern of nineteenth-century urbanizaton was based on nineteenth-century technology. This led to high population densities by reason of the centripetal forces set in motion by the steam engine, the belt and pulley and the horse-drawn vehicle. Twentieth-century technology, in contrast, symbolized by electric power, the telephone and the automobile, generates centrifugal forces which produce a wider dispersion of urban population over the countryscape.

There is great variation, of course, in the extent to which the LDCs can avail themselves of twentieth-century technology. But its potential for affecting spatial patterns in LDC cities must be recognized.

Role of planning. In the MDCs, urban growth was largely the product of the play of free market forces which determined plant location, job opportunity, residential areas and the like. Although central and local government played some role in the planning of urban growth in the MDCs, the role of government was, on the whole, relatively minor. In contrast in the LDCs, given the situation in which they find themselves, much more emphasis is being laid on planning urban growth, and the play of market forces is relatively weak. There is considerable variation, of course, within the LDCs in the actual mix of government planning and the play of market forces, but it is clear that the government role is much more important in urbanization in the LDCs than it was in the MDCs.

Population/Resource Ratios

When the MDCs experienced their economic takeoffs and rapid urbanization, their populations were relatively sparse in relation to their various resources, and increased population growth rates often led to economies of scale and economic growth. In contrast in the LDCs, as they entered the threshold of economic takeoff and as they have experienced rapid urbanization, their populations have been much larger in relation to resources. Given the dominant position of agriculture in many LDCs, rapid population growth contributed more to diminished returns than to economies of scale. Many of the chronic and acute urban problems in the LDCs are much more intractable in their setting of poverty than was the case in comparable stages of urbanization in the MDCs.

World Political Situation

The contemporary world political situation differs in many respects from that which provided the climate for the development of urban places in the MDCs. Especially since the end of World War II, at least two basic changes have occurred that are undoubtedly affecting the curse of urbanization in the less developed countries; these changes were not paralleled in the experience of cities in the West. These are, first, the 'revolution of rising expectations' which has swept the world and which has led the governments and populations of the LDCs to strive for economic development to achieve higher levels of living. Moreover, the LDCs have achieved various forms of organization, including that of the non-aligned nations, which are aggressively pressing for what they perceive to be their fair share of the earth's bounty. Among the specific forms of pressure being applied to the more developed nations to help the LDCs to achieve higher levels of living is their demand for a New International Economic Order (NIEO).[8] Without question, these developments are exerting great influence on the course of events in the LDCs, and they are certainly resulting in more direct intervention in the process of urbanization on the part of governments in the LDCs.

Second, unlike the situation which obtained during the rapid urbanization experienced in the MDCs, especially during the nineteenth century, the world now has many more international organizations, public and private, providing the developing regions with stimulation, technical assistance and capital. Such organizations are undoubtedly affecting the urbanization proc-

41 –

ess. Various agencies of the United Nations are helping the LDCs to cope with problems of rapid urbanization, and in addition there are a number of bilateral and multilateral arrangements leading toward the same end. Finally, a role is played by the great foundations in the MDCs in their various types of programmes to assist the LDCs to achieve development.

Also playing an important role in urbanization in the LDCs is the contemporary world economic order characterized by 'have' nations and 'have-not' nations. The have-not nations, the LDCs, have a subordinate role in their relations with the have nations, whether 'capitalistic' or 'socialistic'. The demand for NIEO is designed to improve the status of the LDCs in the interdependent world economic order in trade, in financial matters, in technology transfers and in power relationships in general. Clearly the subordinate economic and political position of the LDCs adversely affects their ability to plan, to guide, to control and to improve the urban place and the quality of life of their urban inhabitants.[9]

Consequences of Urbanization in the MDCs and LDCs

Clearly, differences in the antecedents of urbanization in the LDCs and MDCs may well generate important differences in the types of problems they encounter and the policies and programmes designed to cope with them. Moreover, MDC and LDC differences in the forces and situations affecting urbanization may well lead to significant differences in the consequences of urbanization. These will be considered below within a framework of varying perspectives of the urban place.

Agglomerative living may be viewed from a number of different perspectives, each of which focuses on a facet of the urban place. More specifically, the city may be viewed as a physical construct, as an economic mechanism, as a form of social organization, as a milieu for human behaviour and as a political or governmental unit. From each of these perspectives urban growth and the process of urbanization have significant consequences in both the MDCs and the LDCs, encompassing both positive and negative elements.

The urban place as a physical construct. The inventions of the 'neolithic revolution', including the domestication of plants and animals, enabled humans to abandon a nomadic existence and adopt relatively fixed habitation. Well-developed patterns of construction evolved for housing, water supply, transport, sanitation and other amenities, including structures for the performance of various urban functions essential for agglomerative living.

The environment provided by nature was increasingly transformed to become human-made. Mumford describes the development of the physical city as essentially consisting of the creation of 'containers' varying from vases, jars and vats to villages. The city can thus be viewed as a 'container of containers'.

The size of urban places was restricted by, among other things, available technology and forms of social organization. Early agglomerations of population were perhaps restricted in size by the distance a woman could carry water on foot. Over millennia, technological developments in the movement of persons and goods and evolving forms of social organization enabled human agglomerations to expand indefinitely with 'the removal of limits' and the emergence of 'urban sprawl', metropolis and megalopolis.

The twentieth-century city in the MDCs has become an awesome physical plant both above and below ground. The urban place in the LDCs, however, while meeting minimum standards of technology and organization to permit large population agglomerations, remains relatively primitive in physical infrastructure and urban amenities.

The city as a physical construct reveals a variety of spatial patterns. The spatial pattern of the pre-industrial city has been described by Sjoberg, with its walls, central location of religious and governmental institutions and markets, and pattern of population distribution featuring the elite near the centre and the poor population distributed toward the periphery and even outside the city walls. Within this framework various sectors were often separated by natural barriers or walls, with spatial differentiation by economic function, by ethnicity or race, or by cultural characteristics such as religion or language. Spatial patterning in the modern industrial urban place differs markedly. City walls have

43 –

disappeared. The pattern of population distribution has been reversed in the newer MDCs, with the elite resident in the periphery of the city or in suburbia and exurbia. Functional, ethnic, racial and cultural groupings are still to be found in the modern city. Although not set apart by walls, they may, nevertheless, be in segregated enclaves in varying degrees. In older cities an admixture of spatial patterns exists, reflecting the superimposition of the modern industrial, spatial structure on the older preindustrial pattern,

The evolution of the city's physical plant has both permitted a higher quality of life, especially in the more developed countries, and precipitated serious problems. Some of these problems have impaired the quality of life and remain unresolved, especially in the LDCs.

A major physical problem confronting urban areas in the LDCs is the existence of 'squatter settlements' or 'shanty towns'. Newcomers to the city, predominantly poor, tend to settle in shanty towns as squatters in home-made, makeshift living quarters in areas usually devoid of even minimum urban amenities such as piped water, sewerage and transport. Although cities in the MDCs also often contain slum enclaves with inferior housing and other physical amenities, the MDC slum is far superior to its physical LDC counterpart. Needless to say, the MDC city is in far superior financial shape to cope with its slums than is the LDC city with its shanty towns. In both types of nations, however, the inhabitants of such blighted residential areas are the poorest elements of their respective populations, characterized by limited literacy, low occupational skills and inadequate preparation for urban life. In both the MDCs and the LDCs social blight as well as physical blight pose serious problems of policy and programme.

Finally, it should be observed that in the MDCs as well as the LDCs physical problems remain chronic and from time to time become acute, calling for increased planning in respect to urban design, environmental degradation, housing, the circulation of persons and goods, recreational facilities, and physical plant for the provision of essential urban services.

The urban place as an economic mechanism. The city owes its origin to agricultural economic development; that is, to developments which created a food surplus, a prerequisite to agglomerative living and to the proliferation of the crafts. Once permanent human settlement was achieved, however, it led to significant transformations in economic activity. Large population clumpings permitted a greater division of labour and increased specialization in non-agricultural pursuits. Urban living led to the emergence of new economic activities and concepts, such as work, private property, contracts, money and credit. In the urban setting, new forms of economic stratification emerged, and varying levels of consumption were generated in accordance with differentials in income distribution, leading to the rich, the middle class and the poor. New forms of economic organization also appeared, such as guilds, employers and employees, financial institutions, corporations and unions. New types of economic problems also emerged, such as unemployment and underemployment, child labour, sweat shops and consumer exploitation. Each of the items listed above may be regarded as economic products of agglomerative living.

Perhaps of greatest significance as a product of the urban agglomeration were increased productivity and increased levels of living, especially in the more developed countries. Division of labour and specialization evolved not only in occupations but also in territories – local, regional and national. This, of course, resulted in increased economic interdependence at local, regional, national and international levels. Needless to say, with increased interdependence increased vulnerability inevitably resulted. With the industrial revolution and the emergence of nations, broader markets led to mass production and to intensified competition among nations.

The increase in economic interdependence and vulnerability generated frictions which led to increases in government intervention and regulation within nations and to new forms of international organization. Various forms of government interventionism emerged, as represented by workmen's compensation, unemployment benefits, old age pensions, health insurance programmes – in general to a number of forms of social security.

On the international front new agencies emerged to provide international institutions to help deal with international problems and, in some cases, to lubricate various types of frictions among nations. These agencies included the International Labour Organization (ILO), the United Nations Educational, Scientific and Cultural Organization (UNESCO), the Food and Agricultural Organization (FAO), the World Health Organization (WHO), the International Bank for Reconstruction and Development (World Bank) and the International Monetary Fund (IMF).

As the size of urban agglomerations increased, economies of scale were experienced by the cities themselves as well as by the individual firms located within the cities. Studies focusing on businesses in more developed countries, especially the United States, have concluded that larger cities have higher productivity in the manufacturing industries. Studies of the impact of city size on productivity are not as readily available for the less developed countries, but there are apparently higher wages in larger places, which suggests higher productivity.

It would seem that there is a point beyond which size may result not in economies of scale but in diseconomies, disamenities and dissocialities. Studies have been made of the relative cost of public service and social and economic infrastructure by city size. Most of such studies have concluded that the economies of scale in municipal services occur in populations up to the range of 100,000–300,000 people. Above this level, it seems that economies may continue for some types of services and not for others. It appears that the vertically integrated services provided by cities experience economies of scale well into population sizes in the millions. This would hold for functions such as those involved in water treatment plants, pipelines, canals, sewage disposal, and gas and electricity supply. Large populations are also required to effect economies in public transportation. While such economies seem definitely to be available to the more developed countries, there is some question as to whether the same situation obtains in the less developed countries, where there may be shortages of capital, ineffective urban planning and inadequate foreign exchange. Available studies indicate that in horizontally integrated services, such as police and fire protection, hospitals and schools, cost curves flatten after the size of 200,000 or so has been reached.[10]

Within the LDC cities, at least three economic sectors are clearly discernible as the pace of urbanization accelerates. These are the 'traditional' sector, which includes pre-industrial forms of economic activity; the 'modern' sector, which contains largely twentieth-century forms of economic organization and functions, often imported from the MDCs; and the 'transitional' or 'informal' sector, which bridges the other sectors. The informal sector is generally concentrated in the squatter, shanty-town areas – the areas of first settlement of new in-migrants. There is increasing awareness that the informal sector, frequently regarded as a pariah element of the economy and society, is truly a transitional sector in both the economic and social orders. As such it may be regarded as an area of opportunity for both economic development and social change towards modernity.

On the positive side, urban living has greatly increased the quality of life by providing higher levels of living and a stimulus to the development of science and technology, to mass literacy and education, to libraries, museums and to the performing arts. Urban living has enriched life in greatly increasing the options available to urban inhabitants. On the other hand, urban living has generated new and difficult problems – physical, economic, social and political. It has been accompanied by increases in environmental degradation: air, water and noise pollution; poverty, consumer exploitation and recession and depression; greatly increased personal and institutional pathology as represented by increased juvenile delinquency, crime, alcoholism, drug addiction, suicide, prostitution and family disorganization; and political and governmental problems such as represented by conflicting governmental jurisdictions, inefficient bureaucracy, abuse of power and corruption.

In general, then, population agglomeration, living in an urban place, has transformed the way in which humans make a living, and this in turn has had and is still having great impact on the entire life space.

The urban place and social organization. Social organization has necessarily also been transformed by reason of changes in the physical city and in the urban economy. In the MDCs, as was noted by Durkheim long ago, social cohesion in the urban setting is increasingly 'organic' rather than 'mechanical', that is, the product of interdependence rather than through the operation of a homogeneous culture. The individual worker's role changes from 'status' to 'contract'. The basic social institution, the family, has, in the MDCs, undergone great modification in the urban milieu. It may be considered as an example of how the urban milieu affects social organization. Many of the traditional functions of the family in the pre-urban setting, as Ogburn recognized, disappear or experience modification and attenuation. More specifically, the family in the MDC urban setting has tended to lose its function as a production unit and increasingly even as a consumption unit. It has lost much of its socialization function in the rearing of the child to a nesting of schools from pre-nursery to university, to peer groups, to the mass media and to libraries and museums. The family's affectional function has become attenuated as evidenced by increased divorce, separation and remarriage. The family protection functions have been taken over by new institutions, such as the police, hospitals, welfare programmes and various social security provisions. The recreational function of the family has largely been taken over by commercial institutions—the cinema, the radio and television, and by commercialized sporting events. In the MDCs the traditional religious functions of the family have become increasingly attenuated in the urban setting, as has the role of the church and religiosity in general.

Finally, it is to be noted that in the urban MDCs the role of women has been greatly modified. Women increasingly have assumed new roles as human beings instead of being merely females with roles restricted to those of wife and mother. Moreover, the relationship between parents and children has been greatly changed as children are increasingly subjected to influences outside the home, and parenting requires significant adjustments.

The types of family transformation described are, of course, primarily evident in the MDCs, but they may well point to what lies ahead in the LDCs as increased urbanization leads to 'urbanism as a way of life'.[11]

In the MDC urban setting, new institutions have emerged by 'enactment' rather than by the slow product of group experience. Examples are almost endless, but a few American ones may be cited to demonstrate the point: the social security system, the

Public Health Service, the Federal Trade Commission, and the Pure Food and Drug Administration.

Bureaucracy, though much decried, has been the inevitable product or urban living; it is a form of complex organization essential for effecting co-ordination and integration of urban functions in every sphere of life, including the economic, social, educational, religious and political ones. The mass society in the urban setting could not function without bureaucracy. It is not possible to abolish it, but it is undoubtedly possible to control it.

Finally, in the urban setting in the MDCs stratification has become based on three axes: status, based on birth; power, based on wealth and income; and prestige, as achieved through intellectual and occupational pursuits. The first axis is a survival from the pre-urban society; the second assumes new forms in the urban setting; and the third is increasingly a product of the urban milieu. Power and prestige as achieved in the urban situation tend increasingly to make status based on birth less important. In the LDCs, status and power tend to be more closely linked than in the MDCs.

The changes in social organization brought by urban living also have positive and negative elements which will be further discussed below in their impact on human behaviour.

The urban place and human behaviour. In the urban setting, the potential of human interaction is greatly increased over that in the pre-urban milieu. To the extent that the potential in increased interaction is realized, it appears that human behaviour is greatly affected. Increases in human interaction may indeed produce as much impact in the realm of the social as a mutation produces in the realm of the genetic. More specifically, a greatly increased number of contacts with others tends to change the nature of the interaction. The classic statement of the effect of increased size and density of population, as well as increased heterogeneity, was made by Louis Wirth.[12] According to Wirth the small community is characterized by 'primary group' contacts that tend to be face-to-face, intimate, and across most of the life space. With such contacts, personal relations are based on full knowledge of the other person, on sentiment and emotion. In

49 –

contrast, in the large, high-density population situation characterized by numerous contacts, the interaction tends to be 'secondary' rather than primary, that is, segmental rather than integral, and utilitarian rather than sentimental. Moreover, in the urban setting contacts increasingly are made with people of different cultures, and the person is therefore subjected to a great variety of values and alternative forms of thought and action.

In such a situation, human behaviour tends to become 'rational' as contrasted with 'traditional', that is, many realms of life become subject to decision-making as contrasted with adherence to the socially inherited *mores* and folkways. In consequence of increases in size and density of population, especially if accompanied by heterogeneity, the power of informal social controls is greatly diminished. Social control becomes increasingly formal, through the law, regulation and fiat and as enforced by the police, courts and jails. Breakdowns in informal social control are largely responsible for greatly increased personal disorganization as manifested in juvenile delinquency, crime, prostitution, alcoholism, drug addiction, suicide, mental disease, social unrest and political instability. It is clear that formal controls have by no means proved as efficacious as informal controls in regulating behaviour.

The modifications in human behaviour described above are, of course, much more in evidence in the MDCs than in the LDCs, although they are certainly emergent in the latter. The reason urban populations resident in the LDCs do not manifest these changes in human behaviour may be traced to the difference in the extent to which potential increase in human interaction that large population size and density permit is actually realized. Cities in the LDCs, much more than in the MDCs, tend to be made up of a number of enclaves–racial, ethnic, religious, linguistic and functional–with minimal contacts among them. To the extent that these enclaves do not engage in social interaction the city is more an agglomeration of units of relatively small size than an integral large and dense population agglomeration. In the relatively small enclave, with social contact restricted largely to other persons within, the common social heritage–including institutions, the folkways and *mores,* values, forms of thought and behaviour–may remain intact in the same number as they do in

-50

an isolated village. As division of labour and economic interdependence increase, however, social interaction with the members of other enclaves may be expected to increase, and increased population size and density may then tend to have the
same consequences as those described for the MDCs.

Finally, it should be noted that population heterogeneity, when
accompanied by increased social interaction, provides a matrix
for accelerated social change, intergroup frictions and both the
positive and negative results of a pluralistic society. In the presence of diverse cultures, increased social interaction tends to
stimulate change in each of the interacting cultures and to contribute to the emergence of a 'melting pot' culture. Free and
unrestricted interaction of culturally diverse peoples had inevitably led to accelerated change, as evidenced in such historical
centres of this interaction as Asia Minor and Central America, as
well as in modern cities in the MDCs.

In initial stages in the interaction of peoples of diverse race,
ethnicity and culture, frictions may be generated, especially
when accompanied by differences in opportunity, levels of living
and power. Such frictions are in evidence in 'communal conflict'
in many parts of the world–in the MDCs as well as in the LDCs.
In the urban setting, pluralistic societies proliferate and undergo
often difficult periods of adjustment and acculturation. In such
pluralistic societies diversity of cultures may on the one hand
stimulate new and exciting forms of thought and behaviour;
but on the other hand pluralistic societies may be fraught
with intense tensions, overt conflicts and extreme forms of
violence.

As the cities in the LDCs become 'modernized' it may be
expected that they will grow more economically interdependent,
and that intergroup social interaction will increase. Increased
modernity in LDC economies is generally desired because of
anticipated increased productivity and higher levels of living. In
many LDCs there is expressed the desire to retain their traditional values and institutions even while gaining the advantages
of increased productivity. The evidence, however, indicates that
it is a forlorn hope that the advantages of urban modernity can be
gained without simultaneously experiencing rapid social change
and transformations of the traditional social heritage.

51 –

The urban place as a unit of government. It has been indicated that agglomerative living in its earliest form required, among other things, emergence of new forms of social organization. It was necessary to have a mechanism for the distribution of the agricultural surplus that made aggregative living possible. It was also necessary to provide minimum defence, police and welfare functions, and functions relating to religion and the spiritual life of the people. Increasing size and density of the population, with growing interdependence and increased vulnerability, inevitably led to the emergence of new functions to be exercised by central authority. Urbanism as a way of life led inexorably to the expansion of government functions and powers, a process by no means yet complete.

National governments both in the MDCs and LDCs vary from those with strong central authority to those with great decentralization. City governments in both the MDCs and LDCs vary in the extent to which they are subject to central government authority and control, and in the extent to which local government leadership is achieved through appointment or popular election. Finally, city governments vary also in structure and procedures. Despite these variations, however, city populations everywhere require essential public services–physical, social and economic. That is, the urban place necessarily requires infrastructure investments for urban amenities including potable water, sewerage or other means of sanitation, housing, transport and recreation. Provision must also be made for public safety, health and welfare; for effective conduct of industry and business which provide employment; and for the maintenance of external relations–with the city hinterland, the region, the nation, and, for some cities, with the world at large.

Increasing urbanization has led to complex and often technical requirements for 'governing'. Urban problems, whether physical, economic, social or political, have increasingly required professional attention of the type that is provided by 'experts' to emerge as a new and powerful element in government. As has been noted above, increased size and density of population have required the development of bureaucracy–a formal organization without which complex problems of urban living could not possibly be resolved.

Increased interdependence on a local, regional, national and international level has created new problems of relationships among governments and organizations on those different levels. In greatly decentralized systems, as in the United States, there has been an increasing tendency for direct relationships to develop between central government and municipal government. In greatly centralized systems, such as in Latin America, there has been a tendency for municipalities to seek greater autonomy. In general, however, there seems to be a general tendency for higher governmental authorities to retain or to achieve increasing powers of control over local governments.

Accelerating urban growth and increased size of city populations have generated strains on local governmental structures throughout the world. Inherited forms of local government have been increasingly unable to cope with metropolitan areas, and this led to various types of new structures in local government, varying from overlays such as represented by port authorities, sanitation districts and the like, to the emergence of metropolitan area government.

Among the types of conflicts that are manifest within metropolitan areas are the conflicts arising from different local jurisdictions between places of residence and places of work, places of shopping, places of recreation, places of schooling and the like. In varying degrees, as certainly is evident in the United States, the strains include those arising from the fact that the need for municipal services is increasingly not consonant with the ability of the population within the city to pay for the services.

In general, it may be stated that the differentiation of function and problems of interdependence and vulnerability arising in urbanism as a way of life exacerbate frictions produced by the disparity between twentieth-century clumpings of people and economic activities and inherited local governmental structures. These frictions are especially acute in areas where, by reason of spatial patterning of the type indicated above, more affluent populations living in suburbia or exurbia outside the city limits leave the central city with poorer populations requiring increased urban services even as their tax base erodes.

Also emergent as one aspect of increased urbanization are the political conflicts of interest between the central city and suburban populations, and between metropolitan area and rural populations, reflected in legislative conflict in democratic forms of government in the MDCs. In the LDCs, in which strong centralized authority tends to obtain, cities–especially the capital cities –may exert disproportionate control over the entire nation by reason of their strategic location in the economy and the government, and get more than their share in the allocation of scarce resources for development.

Concluding Observations

Among the most dramatic and significant developments affecting human affairs during the twentieth century has been and still is the extraordinary increase in the number and proportion of persons living in urban areas. In 1900 it is estimated that there were 218 million persons living in urban places, 13.6 per cent of the world's total population.[13] In 1980 it is estimated that the number of urban inhabitants had increased to 1,807 million, and that the proportion of total population resident in urban places had increased to 41.3 per cent. By the century's end, it is projected by the United Nations that there will be 3,208 million persons inhabiting urban areas, constituting over half of the world's peoples. Thus in the course of the twentieth century, urban residents will have increased fourteenfold and the proportion of the world's population living in urban places will have increased from less than 14 per cent to more than 50 per cent. By 2000 over four-fifths of the people in the MDCs and over two-fifths of those in the LDCs will be resident in urban places. In the LDCs this will result from a near tripling in urban population in the little more than one human generation between 1970 and 2000.

Among the more significant findings on differential urban growth and urbanization between the more developed and less developed countries is the much more important role that natural increase plays in LDC urban growth. While rural-to-urban migration also poses problems for LDC governments, more important than migration is the excess of births over deaths, a major consideration in efforts to dampen urban growth rates. With mortality rates still declining in the LDCs, the need to control high fertility as a means of controlling urban growth becomes even greater. In this connection,it is to be emphasized that evidence is mounting that the birth rate is a mutable factor in the LDCs– family planning is having a significant impact on fertility decline.[14] Urban planning, therefore, on whatever level of government, national, regional or local, must include population policy as an integral element of social and economic policy relating to urbanization.

Only recently has the United Nations begun serious consideration of urbanization in relation to economic development. In discussing the second United Nations Development Decade, the UN Department of Economic and Social Affairs made the following statement:

> The significance of the now universal phenomenon of urbanization has unfortunately only recently been recognized as posing one of the major economic and social problems in developing and developed nations alike. It might have been expected that urbanization would be more of a contributor and less of a problem to contemporary development, as was the case of European and North American cities in the nineteenth century. However, the powerful cause and effect role of urbanization in development is just beginning to be understood.[15]

The same report states the findings of a UN seminar as follows: 'The process of urbanization must be understood as a basic condition for and as a functional consequence of economic, social and technological development. Indiscriminate efforts to avoid urbanization may only serve to delay development.'[16]

Urbanism as a way of life has already profoundly transformed values, institutions, social control, human behaviour, economic activity and organization and the role of government in the more developed countries where the processes are still underway. Urbanization will undoubtedly have increased impact on the cultures and the inhabitants in the less developed countries.

To the extent that urbanism becomes the way of life of over half of the world's population by the century's end, the world may undergo in the next several decades the most radical change in social, economic and political life ever experienced in so short

55 –

a time. This unprecedented happening may well call for unprecedented response by the peoples and governments in both the MDCs and LDCs in the years that lie ahead.

How the Estimates Were Derived

Wherever possible, statistics were taken unchanged from published or unpublished United Nations sources. Because of changes in the United Nations estimates, however, and because of changes in city-size groupings, some figures had to be estimated. The basis for the figures is explained below.

For the years 1920–40, the figures given in *The Growth of the World's Urban and Rural Population, 1920–2000* (United Nations Population Studies No. 44, 1969, hereafter referred to as GWURP) were assumed to be correct for the city sizes and for the urban and total populations. For the years 1960–2000, total population estimates are from *World Population Trends and Policies* (United Nations Population Studies No. 62, 1977, hereafter referred to as WPTP).

Estimates of the population in urban places of various sizes for the years 1950–2000 are from 'Patterns of Urban and Rural Population Growth', Chapter 4 of United Nations Population Studies No. 68 (ST/ESA/SER. A/68), hereafter referred to as PURPG. Estimates for the years 1960–2000 were accepted as correct and those given here for 1950 were derived from interpolation of figures from GWURP and PURPG.

A number of estimates were derived through other procedures. GWURP contains estimates of the population living in places of 20,000+ persons, but no other source uses this grouping. Estimates for such places for the years 1950–2000 were obtained by assuming that the fractions of the total urban populations living in places shown in GWURP were correct; these fractions were applied to the appropriate urban populations from PURPG.

PURPG does not give projections for cities 100,000+ for 1980–2000, nor for cities 250,000+ for 1990–2000 or cities 500,000+ for the year 2000. However, an earlier United Nations source (*Trends and Prospects in Urban Agglomerations, 1950–2000, as Assessed in 1973–1975*, ESA/P/WP. 58, 1975, hereafter referred to as TPPUA) gives figures for cities of 100,000–200,000,

200,000–500,000 and 500,000–1,000,000. To estimate the numbers in cities of 250,000–500,000, an assumption was used based upon the rank-size rule, which indicates that 24 per cent of persons living in cities in the 200,000–500,000 range should be living in cities of between 200,000 and 250,000. Next, ratios were obtained of estimates of the number of persons living in cities of at least the lowest-size category given in PURPG and the numbers living in all urban places as given in PURPG with comparable figures from TPPUA. The difference between the ratios was evenly apportioned throughout the size categories to be estimated. For example, if for the year 2000 the urban population for a given region as shown in PURPG was 1.005 times that given in TPPUA, whereas the comparable figure for the population living in places of 1,000,000 + was 1.025, estimates for the populations living in cities sized 100,000 + , 250,000 + and 500,000 + were derived by multiplying the TPPUA figures by 1.010, 1.015 and 1.020, respectively.

A slight deviation from this procedure was used for estimating the above populations for the more and less developed countries for the years, 1980–2000. The populations of the Soviet Union, North America, Europe and Oceania were first added together for the appropriate years. The population for Japan was then estimated from TPPUA and added to the above sums. These new figures become the population estimates for the MDCs. Estimates for the LDCs were obtained by subtracting the MDC estimates from the world estimates.

Notes

1. Louis Wirth, 'Urbanism as a Way of Life', *American Journal of Sociology* 44 (July 1938): 1–24.
2. United Nations, Department of Economic and Social Affairs, *Growth of the World's Urban and Rural Population, 1920–2000*, Population Studies No. 44 (ST/SOA Series A/44) 1969; United Nations, Department of Economic and Social Affairs, *Patterns of Urban and Rural Population Growth*, Population Studies No. 68 (ST/ESA/Series A/68) 1980, Chapter 4, 'Patterns of Growth Among Cities'.
3. The figures cited below are derived from *Patterns of Urban and Rural Population Growth, op. cit.,* particularly Chapter 3, 'Components of Urban and Rural Population Change', and form pp. 25–35, 208, and Tables 3.2 and 4.6.

4. Daniel R. Vining, Jr and Thomas Kennedy, 'Population Dispersal from Major Metropolitan Regions: An International Comparison', *International Regional Science Review* 3, No. 1 (1978): 49–73; Lester Brown, 'The Limits to Growth of Third World Cities', *The Futurist* 10 (December 1976): 308–15.

5. See for example, Calvin Beale, *Revival of Population Growth in Non-Metropolitan America,* Economic Research Service Bulletin ERS-605 (Washington, DC: US Department of Agriculture, 1975); Richard L. Morrill, 'Population Redistribution, 1965–1975', *Growth and Change* (Lexington, Ky) 9 (April 1978): 35–43.

6. *Ibid,* Chapter 4, p. 47.

7. This section is largely an adaptation and updating of Philip M. Hauser, 'Urbanization: An Overview', in *The Study of Urbanization,* ed Philip M. Hauser and Leo F. Schnore (New York: John Wiley and Sons, 1965), pp. 1–47. The main bibliography can be found there, on pp. 41–7. New sources are listed below.

8. Philip M. Hauser, 'Introduction and Overview,' in *World Population and Development,* ed Philip M. Hauser (Syracuse: Syracuse University Press, 1979), pp 27–37.

9. Roger D. Hansen, *The United States and World Development: Agenda for Action* (New York: Praeger, Overseas Development Council, 1976).

10. United Nations, *Patterns of Urban and Rural Population Growth, op. cit.,* Chapter 4, pp 2–3, 6, 7–8.

11. Wirth, 'Urbanism as a Way of Life', *op. cit.*

12. *Ibid.*

13. United Nations, *Determinants and Consequences of Population Trends* (New York: United Nations, 1973), Vol. 1, pp 21 and 188. 'Urban' here is only taken to mean places of at least 5,000 population. Elsewhere we refer to 'urban' as defined according to each nation's own criteria.

14. Hauser, 'Urbanization', *op. cit.,* pp. 9–12.

15. United Nations, Department of Economic and Social Affairs, *Urbanization in the Second United Nations Development Decade* (New York: United Nations, 1970), pp 1–2.

16. *Ibid,* p. 3.

–2–

Issues and Instruments in Metropolitan Planning

APRODICIO A. LAQUIAN
De la Salle University

Introduction

Since human settlements evolved some 10,000 years ago, society has always found security and fulfilment in large towns. The city has reflected humankind's most tangible achievements and levels of development: the highest achievements in building, production, religion and the arts are enshrined in the city; a people's very sense of values is reflected in city life. The highest accolade a society can give to members is to make them citizens–those of the city.

Of late, the developmental role of cities has come under question. Cities, it is said, have become too large: they have outgrown the human scale; there are too many slums, too much pollution and waste, too much noise. The symbol of the city has changed from the graceful spire of a cathedral to the squarish monolith of an office tower.

This ambivalence about cities has always been a feature of human history: from Aristotle's *Politics* to Chaplin's *Modern Times,* the uneasy relationship between human beings and machines has been a recurrent theme. People concerned about the human condition have worried that the man-made city could become so mechanized that it would be dehumanized. While machines made possible the concentration of economic activities that sustained development, the same technological marvels could despoil the human habitat. Bureaucracies and complex organizations could reduce the human being to the insignificance of a cipher.

These fears notwithstanding, urban agglomerations are still the most efficient mechanisms for accomplishing complex, gigantic, and productive tasks. The need to grapple with large numbers is a challenge to human managerial abilities. 'God created the earth and man built cities,' went a medieval boast. It is in the tradition of large human settlements that adversity only makes people more resilient and inventive. The citizens of Warsaw, for example, rebuilt their beautiful city from the ashes of war; the people of San Francisco constructed a better city from rubble left by an earthquake.

The Growth of Cities

The pervasive influence of cities all over the world at present makes us forget that urbanization is a relatively recent event in the evolution of human society. Jericho, the oldest known town, was founded some 8,000 years ago. The Sumerian cities, with populations that probably reached no more than 20,000, flourished 5,000 or 6,000 years ago. In 600 BC Babylon contained some 80,000 people. The entire city-state of Athens probably had 100,000 people, only one-fifth of whom were real urban dwellers. In the first century AD Rome attained a million population. Canton had 1.2 million by 1800 and London became the first western metropolis to reach a million shortly after that date.[1]

In 1900 there were only 20 metropolitan areas that had a population of one million or more. The combined population of these cities (about 24 million) made up 1.5 per cent of the global population. By mid-century there were 95 cities of a million or more, with a combined population of 205 million, comprising 8.2 per cent of the world's population. At present, 225 cities with a combined population of 631 million make up 14.0 per cent of the global population (Table 2.2). More than half of these cities are in

Table 2.1. Urban Population as Share of Total Population in Selected Countries

Country	Total Population 1972 (in millions)	Urban Population as Share of Total Population 1972 (per cent)	1975
Argentina	23.9	77.4	79.9
Brazil	28.9	55.0	59.4
Canada	22.0	76.0	78.0
People's Republic of China	800.7	22.0	25.0
Colombia	22.5	57.1	61.6
Egypt	34.8	44.0	48.0
France	51.7	73.0	76.0
Federal Republic of Germany	61.7	81.0	83.0
India	563.5	20.0	21.0
Indonesia	121.6	17.0	19.0
Iran	30.6	41.0	44.0
Italy	54.4	64.0	67.0
Japan	107.0	53.0	57.0
Kenya	12.1	10.0	11.0
Democratic People's Republic of Korea	14.7	38.0	43.0
Republic of Korea	32.4	42.0	47.0
Mexico	52.6	59.3	63.1
Nigeria	58.0	16.0	18.0
Peru	14.5	53.8	57.1
Philippines	39.0	33.0	35.0
Thailand	36.3	15.0	16.0
Turkey	37.0	38.0	43.0
Soviet Union	247.5	57.0	61.0
United Kingdom	55.8	78.0	78.0
United States	209.0	74.0	75.0

SOURCE: United Nations, *1974 Report on the World Social Situation* (New York: United Nations, 1975), pp. 36, 57–8, 116–17, 171–2.

less developed countries, including 13.9 million in Mexico City, 12 million in Shanghai, and 9.6 million in Calcutta.[2] The world's urban population, now 42 per cent of the total, will be more than half of the estimated 6.4 billion people expected to be alive in the year 2000.[3]

Implications of Metropolitan Growth

As we enter the 1980s, only two decades from a world that would be half urban, it may be instructive to inquire what urbanization trends imply for world development. Urban growth rates in less developed countries would result in a doubling of large city populations by 1990. It is projected that among urban populations,

Table 2.2. Increase in Number of Million-size Metropolitan Areas, 1870–2000

Year	Total Metropolises	Metro Population (in millions)	World Population (in millions)	Percentage of World Population in Metro Areas
1870	7	13	1,300	1.0
1900	20	24	1,600	1.5
1920	30	70	1,800	3.9
1939	57	140	2,250	6.2
1951	95	205	2,500	8.2
1964	140	362	3,200	11.3
1970	157	418	3,621	11.5
1975	181	505	3,921	13.0
1980	225	631	4,500	14.0
1990	322	955	5,346	17.8
2000	414	1,359	6,407	21.2

SOURCES: Richard J. Forstall and Victor Jones, "Selected Demographic, Economic and Governmental Aspects of the Contemporary Metropolis", *Metropolitan Problems, International Perspectives,* ed Simon Miles (Toronto: Methuen, 1970), p. 11; United Nations, *World Housing Survey, 1974* (New York: United Nations, 1976), pp. 142, 149.

Table 2.3. Extent of Squatting and Slum Dwelling in Selected Cities

City	Year	City Population (000)	Slum and Squatters (000)	Percentage of Slums and Squatters to City Population
Ankara	1970	1,250	750	60
Bangkok-Thonburi	1970	3,041	600	20
Bogotá	1969	2,294	1,376	60
Bombay	1971	6,000	2,475	41
Buenos Aires	1970	2,972	1,486	50
Calcutta	1971	8,000	5,328	67
Caracas	1974	2,369	1,000	42
Casablanca	1971	1,506	1,054	70
Dacca	1973	1,700	300	35
Delhi	1970	3,877	1,400	36
Hong Kong	1969	3,617	600	17
Istanbul	1970	2,247	899	40
Jakarta	1972	4,576	1,190	26
Karachi	1971	3,428	800	23
Kinshasa	1969	1,288	733	60
Lima	1970	2,877	1,148	40
Manila	1972	4,400	1,540	35
Mexico City	1966	3,287	1,500	46
Nairobi	1970	535	177	33
Pusan	1969	1,675	527	31
Rio de Janeiro	1970	4,855	1,456	30
Santiago	1964	2,184	546	25
Seoul	1969	4,600	1,320	29

SOURCES: United Nations, *World Housing Survey* (New York: United Nations, 1976), Table 48, pp. 159–64; *Housing Asia's Millions* (Ottawa: IDRC, 1979), Table 8, p. 53.

those living in slum and squatter areas would be doubling their numbers every five to seven years. Already some cities have shanty-towns that comprise 50-60 per cent of their population (Table 2.3). While the rapid growth of slum and squatter areas has been traditionally due to rural-urban migration, there is some evidence that natural growth processes are playing an increasingly important role in the growth of this particular population segment.

Population projections, of course, are not predictions, and they do not necessarily come true. The inter-relationships among demographic variables and development factors are complex. Continued high rates of population growth might create problems that might serve as a brake on population increase. Urban misery might discourage more people from having more children. Intense overcrowding might contribute to lower fertility. The evidence on these trends is not conclusive, as it is based largely on impressionistic observations of urban poverty and on experiments on the behaviour of Norway rats.

Students of population hope that a 'demographic transition' will prove to be a means of limiting population growth. In its broadest and most uncomplicated outlines, this theory holds that solid economic development, with concomitant improvements in income, health, literacy and education, and with an enhanced economic role for women, would slow down population growth. Improved means of communication, coupled with the availability of contraceptive devices through family planning programmes, would encourage couples to limit and space their families. The higher cost of bringing up children might help to reduce their number. As more and more people live in cities, the transition to smaller families might also occur. It is important to emphasize that current population projections of metropolitan growth need not be self-fulfilling. A Mexico City of 31.2 million or a Sao Paulo of 26 million (by the year 2000) is not an inevitability. Such projections and the urban problems implied by them need not paralyze us to inactivity. Rather, they should serve as warning signs and a rationale for intervention that may prevent negative metropolitan trends.

It is tempting simply to extrapolate from population growth

trends and translate growth rates into requirements for potable water, transportation, shelter, food and other basic needs. A simulation model for Madras, India, did precisely this in 1960.[4] Starting from a base population of 2 million in 1960, the model tried to estimate the volume of basic needs required by each jump in population. The model indicated that by the time the population of Madras reached 32 million (in 2000), the city would run out of fresh water. The automobile would have to go; bicycles and para-transit modes would be more appropriate. Food would have to be produced within the city, most of it in urban villages occupied by recent migrants. Houses would be self-built, based on simple designs that unskilled people can execute. The model indicated environmental collapse by the time population reached 60–80 million. Physical space for outward expansion would simply run out. Ethnic riots and serious political upheavals would become a distinct possibility. Most critically, collapse and disorganization would be possible before the population stabilized and zero population growth was achieved.

The Madras model projected a population of 32 million by the year 2000. Estimates currently available expect a population of 10.6 million by that date. Does this mean the model was wrong and there is really nothing to worry about? Were there internal dynamics in the development of Madras that prevented the population from exploding?

To reject the Madras model because it did not precisely predict the rate of population growth is to miss the point. The value of the model lies in its specification of the various needs created by people with such escalation in numbers. An instrument that indicates the magnitudes of water, transport, housing and food demanded by increasing numbers of people is most useful, especially if it goes beyond simple population projections.

In retrospect, it is the failure of the model to go beyond simple population projections that subjects it to criticism. A greater concern with the relationships between the various dimensions of population factors and development variables calls attention to the fact that there are many other demographic variables at play at any one time. As Mr Rafael Salas, Executive Director of the United Nations Fund for Population Activities, has noted:

It is vitally important that all the various population factors, including size, growth, fertility, mortality, migration, urbanization, age structure and spatial distribution continue to be perceived as what they are . . . important variables that act and are acted upon by other factors related to socio-economic and political conditions.[5]

Consideration of these interactions between population variables and socio-economic development factors is what comprehensive planning is all about. In the past, planners simply took population growth figures and tried to estimate the types and magnitudes of physical space, infrastructure investments, and social services required by this growth. Aside from growth, however, there are many other demographic variables that directly or indirectly affect people's needs. As more and more people get added to existing populations, these other factors (migration, urbanization, spatial distribution, changing age structures) have to be considered more seriously.

To illustrate the interaction between population and development factors, consider the estimation of housing needs. The traditional formula for figuring out housing needs considers the following as elements: population size, average size of household, and the number of households that occupy a single dwelling. Since the average size of household in most countries is given and the goal of most housing programmes is to provide one dwelling for each household, the main determinant of housing need turns out to be population size. In other words, the rate of new household formation due to population increase becomes the most important element in the formula.

A more careful analysis of housing need, however, reveals that the demographic variables are only partial dimensions of the phenomenon. The concept of a dwelling, itself, is an important variable because it is culturally determined (a dwelling might be a house, a cave, a tent or a mobile housing unit). The concept also carries with it the judgmental notion of an acceptable dwelling standard. Thus the housing need in a less developed country might be determined by the need to replace sub-standard housing. In the Philippines, an important dimension of the housing need is the replacement of dwellings due to losses from dilapidation as well as from natural or man-made calamities. In Sri Lanka, losses due to obsolescence are important elements in housing need. Singapore also includes losses due to government demolition programmes. The type of materials used in housing, the age of the housing stock, the climatic conditions in a country and the standard used for determining what is acceptable or unacceptable housing obviously help determine the nature of the housing need.

Another element of housing need is the backlog of dwellings required by households that have not been able to find acceptable dwellings in the past. These households might be doubling up with others; new dwellings are needed to thin out densities in existing homes. Again, acceptable densities are culturally determined. In Malaysia, the desired density is four persons per household occupying a single dwelling. By comparison, the median American household in 1970 consisted of 2.6 persons occupying a house with five rooms. The American tendency is toward larger houses for smaller families. Between 1960 and 1970, housing units with six rooms increased by 25 per cent; those with seven rooms or more increased by over 37 per cent. At the same time, the number of non-family households in the United States (single persons living alone, two or more unrelated individuals living together) had been increasing, so that by 1970 they comprised 19 per cent of all United States households. By 1975 the proportion of non-family households had increased to 22 per cent.[6]

While housing needs in the United States are influenced by relatively lavish standards of consumption, those in less developed countries (LDCs) are determined by more basic concerns. For example, many LDCs are still preoccupied with qualitative measures of housing such as providing piped water to every dwelling, including a lavatory and bath in each house, or adding an enclosed kitchen. In some countries the housing shortage is so acute that planners have included in their estimates of housing stock all units used as dwellings, regardless of qualitative conditions. Even at that, figures on housing needs in most LDCs still show a wide gap between demand and supply.

The Role and Scope of Metropolitan Planning

To top executives and council members who govern big cities, futuristic models might not be of much interest. These executives are called upon *now* to provide urban services. Unfortunately, they are expected to deliver these services under conditions of limited authority and power, as well as serious constraints on resources. These are normally lodged in higher levels of government. Despite the fact that tax revenues are generally raised in cities, only a limited share of such resources is spent there. As the growth nodes of development, cities have to share resources with rural areas that often have large populations.

Urban problems are rooted in this partial scope of metropolitan planning. Metropolitan boundaries are often arbitrary lines drawn in space to encompass urbanized and urbanizing areas. Boundary redefinitions, however, can be entangled in local and national political issues. There is an inevitable time-lag between empirical developments and the response of governments. In the case of Greater London, for example, which has gone through a number of boundary changes and metropolitan reforms, Luther Gulick observed that: 'The existence of a fixed and immortal boundary tends to create and sustain a fixed and immortal governmental institution.'[7] Just how impervious to change those boundaries and institutions are may be gleaned from a study of the passage of the Local Government Act which reorganized the Greater London Council. This process started in 1957 and resulted in the passage of the act in 1963. To some extent, the political contests involved in it are still going on.[8]

The service demands within metropolitan jurisdictions are often dictated by factors outside their boundaries. With their limited powers, local executives and local councils do not exert much influence over these forces. They simply receive the brunt of these forces and attempt to accommodate to them as best they can.

Foremost among determinants of urban problems are demographic factors related to metropolitan growth. As pointed out by Hauser and Gardner, urbanization in more developed countries was both 'an antecedent and consequence of increased pro-

APRODICIO A. LAQUIAN

Table 2.4. Percentage of Migrants to Metropolitan Populations in Selected Cities

City	Year	Percentage of Migrants
Abidjan	1963	76
Bandung	1961	43
Bogotá	1966	33
Bombay	1961	52
Caracas	1966	50
Istanbul	1965	50
Jakarta	1968	59
Lagos	1962	75
Nairobi	1969	50
Sao Paulo	1967	68
Seoul	1965	63

SOURCES: United Nations, *World Housing Survey* (New York: United Nations, 1976), Table 44, p. 152; A. Laquian, *Rural-Urban Migrants and Metropolitan Development* (Toronto: Intermet, 1971).

ductivity and higher levels of living'.[9] As cities grew, they attracted migrants from the countryside; technological innovations, specialization, economies of scale and higher productivity made this possible. In most LDCs, however, the very technology that made rapid urbanization possible altered demographic processes as well. Improvements in water supply, sanitation and medical services resulted in less sickness and death, thus accelerating population growth. The widening gap in incomes and opportunities between villages and town engendered rural-urban migration. The migration occurred at the same time that the capital-intensive nature of urban-based production absorbed a smaller proportion of labour.

In most LDC cities, migrants typically constitute from half to three-quarters of metropolitan area populations (Table 2.4); increasingly, these migrants are coming from unskilled segments of rural labour. The weight of their numbers strains urban services to the limit (Table 2.5). Metropolitan authorities, however, are virtually powerless to stop migrants from coming to the city: efforts to close cities to migrants, from Jakarta to Moscow, have been singularly unsuccessful.[10]

Once in the metropolitan area, migrants continue to be quite mobile. Turner and others who have studied urbanization in Latin America have noticed a tendency for migrants to move first to inner-city slums. Once their situation improves, they move to the urban periphery.[11] This process of 'premature suburbanization' has been responsible for the urban sprawl that is seen in met-

Table 2.5. Indicators of Housing Conditions in Urban Areas of Selected Countries

Country	Year	Percentage of Urban Dwellings with 3 or More Persons per Room	Percentage of Urban Dwellings with Piped Water	Percentage of Urban Dwellings with Lavatories
Brazil	1970	4.9	54.4	85.6
Canada	1971	0.1	99.3	100.0
Chile	1970	14.7	–	68.9
France	1968	2.7	97.0	64.2
Greece	1971	–	94.6	98.1
Hong Kong	1971	–	97.2	–
Republic of Korea	1970	–	54.6	92.3
Mexico	1970	–	80.2	61.0
Philippines	1970	–	54.3	–
Singapore	1966	–	91.4	88.7
Sweden	1970	0.1	99.2	–
Thailand	1970	–	47.4	–
United States	1960	–	99.4	98.1

SOURCE: United Nations, *World Housing Survey* (New York: United Nations, 1976), Table 49, pp. 166–72.

ropolitan Lima, greater Rio de Janeiro and the capital district of Mexico. As the migrants move farther and farther into the periphery, they become 'marginalized' in both the spatial and socio-economic sense. Their integration into the economic and political life of the metropolis becomes more difficult.

On quite another plane, the physical ageing of cities in more developed countries (MDCs) is also creating population changes. Typically, the central business district is the first area to age, pushing well-to-do residents toward the suburbs and attracting poorer migrants. Although this pattern of succession was evident in the 1920s (as shown in the classic studies by Park and Burgess of the city of Chicago), the widespread use of the automobile, especially in the period after World War II, accelerated the flight to the suburbs.[12]

In New York City, some 2 million middle-income people have fled the city since the War. They have been replaced by profoundly poor residents, including illegal aliens estimated at half a million to 1.5 million. Since 1947, about 500,000 jobs in manufacturing have disappeared in the city. Of 161 job categories surveyed by the US Bureau of Labor Statistics, 147 have registered declines from 1969 to 1976.[13]

The flight to the suburbs in many American cities also has an

69 –

ethnic dimension. Migrants to suburban areas are predominantly white, while inner-city movers are blacks or Hispanics. The racial tensions created by this phenomenon, typified by the 'long hot summers' of the late 1960s, have simmered down. The differences persist, however, and few people are willing to bet that problems will not recur.[14]

Since 1970 there has been a reversal in urbanization trends in the United States. For the first time in US history more Americans are moving away from metropolitan areas than are moving to them. Falling birth rates in cities and the out-migration of people have halted population growth in many metropolitan areas. There are indications, as well, that urban depopulation is related to ageing of the American population. Most American migrants are going to the 'sunbelt', the region made up of southern and south-western states. This shift in population from the north-east and north central states, the traditional region of large cities, has resulted in dramatic changes in the demographic and socio-economic profiles of both the sending and receiving areas.[15]

The Case for Interventions: Issues and Instruments

The demographic and development patterns mentioned above serve to highlight a number of issues faced by metropolitan planning in both MDCs and LDCs. The in-migration of people which contributes to urban sprawl points to the issue of area-wide jurisdictions. The accelerating demand for urban services focuses on the issue of metropolitan finance. The increasing inability of poorer segments of the population to meet the cost of urban services raises issues related to low-cost housing, transportation systems and services for social development. The proliferation of formal and informal groups in metropolitan society calls attention to the issue of popular participation in urban management. In pursuing each of the issues mentioned above, authorities have evolved instruments to solve them.

Area-wide Jurisdictions

Most large cities of the world suffer from urban sprawl. As urban life spills beyond city boundaries, it engulfs open space, villages, towns and cities. To date, strong traditions of local autonomy result in governmental fragmentation. Although metropolitan areas like Bangkok, Manila, Paris and New York have expanded their area jurisdictions, unified metropolitan governments have not yet been successfully organized. Metropolitan Manila still has 29 local government units despite the reorganization of the metropolitan structure since 1975. The governance of Greater New York is said to involve '1,400 governments' as well as hundreds of special authorities and regional bodies.

Of late, accelerating problems of urban services and intergovernmental relations are bringing about metropolitan reform. In both MDCs and LDCs a number of metropolitan-wide arrangements are being evolved. In these regionally organized systems, urban services are administered over an area which includes the built-up core, semi-urban areas at the periphery, and even the rural hinterland still to be urbanized. These administrative and political arrangements include the following:[16]

(i) Comprehensive local government systems: one or more general-purpose local government systems administers the whole urban region. There may be a single local government, as in Zagreb, Yugoslavia, or a multi-tiered local government structure, as in metropolitan Toronto.

(ii) Multi-jurisdictional systems: the regional organization includes a mixture of central and local governments. The coordinating authority may lie with a central government official such as a prefect or a governor. Examples of this type are the Paris region and metropolitan Manila.

(iii) Field administration systems: regional administration is carried out by a field office of the central government. Examples of this system are the Bangkok municipality and the capital city of Teheran.

The setting-up of area-wide jurisdictions enhances the creative tension between administrative efficiency on the one hand and popular participation on the other. The unification of powers at a regional level clarifies lines of authority. Better co-ordination is also achieved as local interests tending toward fragmentation are subsumed under the general interest. The retention of the lower tiers of government, however, makes popular participation possible. Local officials at lower tiers are more accessible to organized groups, and the presence of representative structures at the grass-roots level encourages a planning process that originates at the bottom.

In most regionally organized systems the role of the central government is usually paramount. In India, for example, local units are subject to a statute that defines their essential and discretionary duties. Definition of the essential duties has improved accountability of local units to the central government. At the same time, clarification of the discretionary duties has encouraged local units to expand their service responsibilities in areas where a special local need or local competence was present.[17]

One advantage of an area-wide approach is that responsibility over urban services may be allocated at appropriate metropolitan, municipal or local levels. For example, the impounding and purification of water may be the responsibility of a regional body, while distribution, system maintenance and collection of user charges might be delegated to lower governmental levels. In the United States, educational facilities are divided among various school boards and governmental units. Facilities that cater to special groups (youth, the aged and infirm, the handicapped) are also provided at various governmental levels in Sweden.

The changing age structures in a metropolitan area exert varying demands on urban services. In most industrialized countries, suburban communities tend to have younger populations. They also have a richer tax base, which assures that excellent educational opportunities exist for children. With the ageing of populations, suburban communities suffer the 'empty nest syndrome', when children move to universities or find jobs elsewhere. The effect of this demographic change in the demand for services is illustrated by the age cohort born between 1947 and 1961 in the United States (the so-called 'baby boom' generation). Median age in the United States is gradually rising, because fewer children are being born to take the baby boomers' place. If present birth rates continue, more than 15 per cent of Americans would be 65 and over by the year 2030. Long before that date, however, many schools would have been closed, maternity and child health clinics reduced in number, and day-care centres phased out. Older populations might return to inner-city areas to enjoy the cultural amenities (theatres, fine restaurants, condominiums) or they might move to 'leisure cities' for retired people in America's sunnier climes.

While older people are looked after by the extended family in third world societies, a more institutional approach tends to be used in MDCs. The siting of 'old folk's homes' among local units in a metropolitan area often creates tension and controversies. Economic reasons favour larger institutions that can be managed more efficiently. However, these large institutions set the old people apart from society and they suffer from the stigma associated with special facilities for the infirm and those awaiting death. Happily, in certain cities smaller institutions have been set up and distributed among various local governments in the metropolitan area. In metropolitan Toronto, for example, homes for the aged are small enough to be functionally integrated into existing neighbourhoods. Old people are able to patronize local markets, participate in community affairs, and otherwise lead normal lives. Because the homes are dispersed all over the metropolitan area, the old people are not too visible and they can function as members of the urban communities.

While demographic changes can demand adjustments in metropolitan functioning, changes in the urban environment can also affect demographic processes. Fertility, for example, is very sensitive to processes that are integral to urbanizaton. Higher levels of income, education and socio-economic mobility might contribute to lower fertility. Even in LDCs, the communication revolution which conveys greater information on family planning might, when combined with better access to contraceptive means, also assist in lowering fertility. These trends are already seen in Singapore and Hong Kong. With the prospects of a world that would be half urban by the year 2000, it is highly possible that the demographic transition would be attained by many more LDCs by that date.

Metropolitan Finance

The capacity of local executives and councils to provide urban services greatly depends on their ability to raise funds. As already mentioned, rural-urban migration contributes to exacerbate the financial problems of metropolitan areas by straining

urban services. The arbitrary delineation of metropolitan boundaries means that people from nearby jurisdictions might avail
themselves of metropolitan services without fully paying for
them. User charges such as tolls or fees may not truly reflect the
extent of metropolitan subsidies. Besides, some migrants attracted to the metropolitan area might simply be too poor to pay
for urban services.

There are, of course, financial opportunities that arise from
rapid urbanization. Enhanced economic activities expand the tax
base. In metropolitan Toronto the expansion of the area jurisdiction of the metropolitan authority to encompass affluent suburbs
has increased the metropolitan unit's credit rating. In Detroit, the
city has been empowered to levy an income tax of one-half of one
per cent a year from people who commute to the city to work
(residents pay a tax of 2 per cent). In metropolitan Manila, industries located within a 50-kilometre radius of the city centre are
taxed 150 per cent higher than those farther out. While this measure is meant to disperse industries, it also provides an excellent
source of revenue to the metropolitan area.

Possibilities for raising metropolitan revenue depend heavily
on relationships between central and regional government. These
relationships follow different patterns in centrally planned and
market-type economies, as well as among MDCs and LDCs. An
interesting trend is that while metropolitan areas in planned
economies and in LDCs are tending toward more local autonomy
and decentralization, the tendency in market-oriented economies
and MDCs is toward greater centralization.[18]

The nature of the relationship between central and metropolitan government is best exemplified in the matter of grants. In a
study of metropolitan areas conducted by the Institute of Public
Administration of New York in 1968, about a quarter of local
authority revenues were derived from direct grants from higher
authorities. In some instances grants covered more than half of
local revenues. Without such grants, shared taxes and other
funds from higher authorities, many cities would find it impossible to meet the demands for services by their increasing populations.[19]

Assistance to metropolitan authorites often takes the form of
an equalization grant system, by which the central government

allocates funds more equitably among different levels of government. In Japan taxes from three national levies (personal income tax, corporate income tax and the liquor tax) are deposited into a local allocation tax system. These funds are allocated to local units according to a formula based on the minimum financial needs of each locality and its standard tax revenues. Each year the central government checks each local government budget and calculates the equalization grant. This calculation is based on:

(i) The size of population, area of the local unit, number of local government employees, number of public school teachers and number of public facilities.

(ii) The unit cost of each public facility or public employee.

(iii) Geographical features such as temperature, location and density of population which might affect local government costs. Local authorities in Japan can apply for block grants from the equalization grant system by calculating the balance between their minimum financial needs and their estimated local revenues. Such grants might amount to 60–80 per cent of expected local revenue. In the case of large cities, higher equalization grants might be possible, depending on estimates of real financial needs.[20]

Region-wide organization, as in the Greater London area, may also create problems of equalization of funds among local units within a regional structure. For many decades a rate equalization fund has been used in allocating funds in Greater London. The system takes the *per capita* average of local incomes as a criterion for assistance. Local areas with *per capita* average income lower than the regional average are given higher priority in assistance. Various methods of weighting may also be included in the basic formula to suit local conditions.[21]

Metropolitan authorities, of course, usually find it more difficult to raise capital investment funds compared to resources needed for current operating expenditures. Here again, the role of higher levels of government is predominant. Local authorities in Australia can borrow capital funds from the Australian Loan Council, while Dutch local authorities can borrow from the Municipal Fund of the Netherlands. Large regional authorities may also obtain loans from banks, insurance companies and other financial institutions. In some rare instances, metropolitan authorities might also obtain loans from international capital markets.

In the final analysis, the financial viability of metropolitan authorities eventually depends on their ability to raise local revenue. A common theory concerning local government taxation is that the devolution of taxing powers to local units would increase revenues because local collectors know the local situation and because citizens would be more willing to pay taxes if they knew it would go to local projects. Studies of local government finance reveal, however, that local officials find it more difficult to gain public assistance in collecting more and higher taxes. Local officials are closer to the public and are more directly affected by local reactions to specific issues. A local official advocating higher local taxes courts political disaster. Because of this, and other factors, most local government authorities do not fully utilize the taxing powers delegated to them by higher government; they find it more convenient to rely on higher government levels to collect revenue, and to share in these proceeds afterwards.

Income from real property taxes remains the most important source of revenue in urban areas. In regional unorganized systems, local authorities might lose revenue by competing with each other for tax revenues. Thus one local unit might assess properties at lower values in order to attract industries, or another might impose a lower rate to do the same. Regional organization would make uniform assessment, fix rates and collect taxes. Area-wide registration of properties, preparation of metropolitan tax rolls and tax maps, cadastral surveys, periodic reassessment of properties to take improvements into consideration, and sustained training of tax personnel are some innovations that a unified approach can make possible to increase real property tax proceeds.

Housing and Services

One area where population pressures continue to create shortages in both MDCs and LDCs is in housing. Limited urban space and spiralling costs of building materials are combining to price housing out of the reach of many families. The World Bank estimated that the percentage of households unable to afford even the lowest cost for a unit of housing was 68 per cent in Nairobi, 64 per cent in Ahmedabad, 63 per cent in Madras, 55 per cent in Mexico City, 47 per cent in Bogotá and 35 per cent in Hong Kong. Even if lower housing standards are used (shared kitchens and sanitary facilities, use of multi-family dwellings), the bottom 25 per cent of urban populations would still be unable to pay for minimal housing in most Asian and African cities.[22]

With very few exceptions (cities in socialist countries are notable examples), metropolitan government is not usually involved in housing. Housing finance is typically a function of higher levels of government, and national housing authorities or housing boards exist at national or provincial levels. In most cases, housing agencies such as the Housing and Development Corporation of Indonesia are granted autonomous powers to raise funds, build housing, manage housing estates and generally engage in the housing business in a corporate manner. Housing finance is also stressed by a number of institutions, for example the Banco Obrero in Venezuela and the Housing Finance Corporation in the Philippines.

Some governments are content to leave housing to the private sector, with the government's role confined to comprehensive planning, providing infrastructures and services, setting housing regulations and standards and making housing loans available. In Sri Lanka, for example, statutes govern the number of houses a family can own, set the amounts of rents that can be charged by a landlord and stipulate the capital gains tax imposed on sale of a dwelling. However, the government does not engage in housing construction, preferring to leave this to the private sector.[23]

In most LDCs the house itself (what is known in ekistics as the shell) is not the most important problem. Indigenous building materials and traditional construction techniques make conventional housing affordable. Difficulties may arise, though, because of the shortage of serviced land. The share of land in shelter provision is about 30 per cent in industrialized countries, with labour and construction materials making up the remainder. In most LDCs the reverse is usually the case: land costs could account for about two-thirds of total housing costs in the Philippines, for example. This state of affairs is the result of faulty land policies and land-use planning, and rampant speculation in land is the major reason behind high costs. Governments are usually unable to recoup social benefits created by public investments which accrue to private landowners. Real estate taxes are not effectively used for increasing municipal revenues and regulating land ownership and land use.

In some less developed countries (Peru, Argentina, Sri Lanka, the Philippines) urban land reform laws have been enacted; these have taken the form of breaking down large holdings and subdividing them into smaller plots, imposing a ceiling on how many houses and lots a family can own, and imposing rent control and capital gains taxes as well as taxes on idle lands. Many of these reforms have had the same mixed results as their rural counterparts. Where those who benefit from the *status quo* are the first ones to be hurt by reform, it is difficult to expect that they would willingly support legislation that would be harmful to themselves.

The main demand on housing has come from the millions of migrants who have flocked to the cities. Finding that housing is beyond their means, some migrants have taken matters into their own hands and squatted on public or private land. The local terms for squatters provide a colourful array of the means for invading property: *paracaidastas* (parachutists) in Mexico; *gecekondu* (night flyers) in Ankara and Istanbul; *barrios piratas* (pirate settlements) in Guayaquil; and *callampas* (mushroom towns) in Santiago. In the beginning, considerable alarm was voiced about the problems and revolutionary implications of this lack of regard for property. Slowly, however, a change in outlook among public officials has come about. Instead of the strict and punitive measures adopted in the beginning, more accommodationist measures are now being used to deal with squatters.

Based on repeated research findings that people in slum and squatter areas have economic and organizatonal resources to provide their own housing, more and more 'self-help' and 'mutual aid' components are being introduced in low-cost housing programmes. Often these are integrated with such activities as digging drainage canals, laying out water and sewerage mains, and constructing and maintaining paths and alleyways where people are expected to provide 'sweat equity'. Housing agencies are also veering away from providing finished houses, preferring 'core housing' approaches where the people are expected to finish the house as their needs and resources make this possible. This has been found to be cheaper and more responsive to people's needs.

An excellent example of a gradualist approach to housing is the programme pursued by the Fundación Salvadorena de Desarrollo y Vivienda Minima (FSVM) in El Salvador. FSVM is a private, non-profit organization but it supplies more than one-fifth of the country's national housing requirements. Its housing programme features a variety of housing types, ranging from a basic serviced site to finished housing for sale or rent. The Foundation realizes that different families have various housing needs; that even the same family's needs change in the course of time. It therefore provides various housing options to respond to these demographic, economic and other changes.

A particularly interesting aspect of FSVM housing is the requirement for participating households to engage in 'mutual aid' activities, such as assisting other families in laying out a house foundation, helping others carry building materials, joining others in digging ditches, and so on. Participating family members have to undergo a training programme in construction techniques. Skills learned are applied in mutual aid or in constructing one's own dwelling. Credit in cash and in the form of building material loans are provided. Technical assistance in house construction and maintenance is also made available. In general, FSVM does not hope to deliver housing to the people; its goal is to tap their resources and energies to provide their own housing by mutual aid and self-help approaches.[24]

One of the most difficult problems in housing is the existence of old and dilapidated structures in inner-city areas (the *bustees* of Bombay and Calcutta, *corralones* of Lima and *tugurios* of Bogotá are typical). Facilities and services in these zones are inadequate or even non-existent. In some instances these slums are so crowded that bed spaces are let out, sometimes in shifts.

The western approach of 'urban renewal' is not applicable to inner-city slums in less developed countries. High densities mean that if they were torn down and replaced with new housing, not all of the former residents could be accommodated in the new houses. Thus in many third world cities programmes of 'community upgrading' are increasingly being initiated. In the Indonesian cities of Jakarta, Surabaya, Bandung, and Yogyakarta the Kampong Improvement Programme mobilizes people through mutual aid projects that include provision of a basic sanitation module (an artesian well, a lavatory and a water reservoir) as well as the laying out and improvement of paths and alleys. In Tondo, Manila, some 250,000 people are benefiting from a community upgrading project supported by the World Bank. In Nairobi's Mathare Valley a similar project is being supported by the European Development Fund. In all these projects a strong community development component is to be found: the people are encouraged and motivated to contribute their personal, financial and organizational resources to the total development effort.

The increasing popularity of self-help approaches is seen in the widespread use of 'sites and services' projects (Table 4.6 cites some examples). Originally, sites and services involved an effort to influence the direction of urbanward migration and to counter urban sprawl. By providing serviced land at the city's periphery,

Table 2.6. World Bank Supported Sites and Services Projects

Project	Specifications	Amounts (in millions of US$)
1. Botswana (1974) Francistown	1,800 sites and services lots; 1,000 dwellings for upgrading; 700 sites and services lots	IDA Credit $3.3
2. El Salvador (1974)	7,000 sites and services lots	IDA Credit $6.0; loan $2.5
3. Indonesia (1974)	18,000 sites and services lots; 1,950 ha. upgrading	IBRD loan $25.0
4. Jamaica (1974)	6,000 sites and services lots; 2,750 dwellings for upgrading	IBRD loan $15.0
5. Republic of Korea (1974)	2,000 sites and services lots	IBRD loan $15.0
6. Nicaragua (1973)	5,900 sites and services lots	IDA Credit $8.0
7. Senegal (1972)	15,600 sites and services lots; 9 ha. upgrading	IDA credit $18.0
8. United Republic of Tanzania (1974)	10,600 sites and services lots; 8,800 dwellings for upgrading	IDA Credit $8.5
9. Zambia (1974)	12,000 sites and services lots; 17,000 dwellings for upgrading	IBRD loan $20.0

SOURCE: IBRD Site and Services Projects Survey and Analysis of Urbanization Standards and On-Site Infrastructure, August 1974.

planers hoped that they would be able to persuade migrants to locate where they were needed. A number of early efforts encountered serious problems. The Pikine project in Dakar, for example, was too far from the city centre and, seven years after its inception, only a handful of people had moved there. The Sapang Palay project in metropolitan Manila did not have enough services or job opportunities, and people relocated there eventually moved back to the inner city. Among the initial problems encountered in sites and services projects were distance from the city, the high cost of transportation, lack of economic opportunities in the relocation site, lack of services, excessively high standards of infrastructure and services, faulty designs in housing and infrastructures, relatively high charges for housing and services, and imposition of rules such as prohibition of using makeshift materials or renting parts of accommodation. Happily, a learning process has occurred in the design and management of these projects and recent projects are more successful.

The first sites and services project supported by the World Bank was launched in 1972. Since then, many lessons have been learned, the most important of which was the wisdom of accommodating to the needs and lifestyles of the poor in designing projects for them. In many countries, it was found that the location of a project is a most important consideration that may outweigh the availability of cheap land in other parts of the city. Resettling people in sites at the urban periphery, unless accompanied by provision of employment opportunities and services, will bring hardships to the urban poor rather than helping them.

Early planners of sites and services projects tended to impose over-ambitious standards. There was a bias toward finished housing and the neat aesthetic lines of homogeneous dwellings. Finished houses, however, cost a great deal more than core housing, and they usually failed to meet the specific needs of people. Later projects have tended to provide only basic shelter, leaving the responsibility for expanding and improving dwellings to the people.

Since 1972 the World Bank has expanded sites and services projects, so that by 1980 there were 32 projects in 26 countries in operation, with another 11 projects in as many countries under consideration. A target of 25 more projects costing about $1 billion (about 7.3 per cent of the Bank's lending programme) has been proposed by 1983.[25] Following the lead of the Bank, other donor agencies such as the US Agency for International Development, the European Development Fund, the Canadian International Development Agency, the Asian Development Bank and others have also launched sites and services and community upgrading projects. It is worth noting that in all these new projects gradualist approaches and self-help are standard requirements.

Even as most countries in the world attempt to accommodate rural-urban migrants in low-cost housing schemes, the potentials for more formal types of housing provision are worth considering. Despite the unique characteristics of development in the city-states of Singapore and Hong Kong, conditions in those two countries provide some lessons for the future.

Before 1960 Singapore had some of the worst slum conditions in south-east Asia. In February of that year the Government created the Housing and Development Board (HDB) to look after public housing construction and management, urban renewal and resettlement. From 1960 to 1975 HDB built some 230,000 units, housing more than one million people or 51 per cent of the entire population. In successive five-year building programmes HDB built so many housing units that by the end of 1980 it is estimated that about 70 per cent of the 2.5 million people of Singapore will be housed in HDB flats.[26]

Hong Kong's housing record is as impressive as Singapore's. Despite the massive in-migration of people from the Chinese mainland, the government has been able to house more than half of the colony's population in public housing. The rest of the people are housed mainly through the efforts of an energetic private sector, ably assisted by government. In the current ten-year public housing programme in Hong Kong (1973–83), housing for 1.8 million people (about 240,000 units) is planned for construction. The plan's objective is to ensure that every family would eventually have a permanent, self-contained home within reach of employment and other facilities at a rent or price it can afford. The government's methods comprise improving the flow of finance to the housing market, building new towns, expanding existing communities, improving or redeveloping the existing housing stock, and providing temporary housing for emergencies and squatter clearances.[27]

Because of the limited land available in Singapore and Hong Kong, multi-storey housing has been favoured. Most public housing is increasingly centred about industrial estates where employment, commerce and social services are clustered together. An important aspect of public housing in Singapore and Hong Kong has been the gradual improvement in standards; in fact HDB in Singapore has now embarked on more expensive housing, catering to the higher incomes and requirements of more prosperous clients. New HDB flats have more and larger rooms and even feature panelled finishes, landscaping and other touches of luxury.

Housing programmes in Singapore and Hong Kong, of course, are heavily influenced by the demographic situation. In Singapore an intensive family planning programme, combined with the socio-economic changes integral to the process of demographic transition, have lowered population growth rates to replacement levels. The current Singaporean family planning programme is not content with the slogan: 'Stop at two', and now insists on proper spacing of children. Communication and exhortation are combined with disincentives that penalize couples with more than two children in the allocation of housing, education and other benefits. Family planning aids are also made available to people through the medical services and other channels.

There are people who argue that conditions in Singapore and Hong Kong are unique and that the housing successes of both countries are not replicable in others. This may be true. However, with population growth rates rising as fast as they do in most less developed countries, densities comparable to those in Singapore and Hong Kong can be expected in the not too distant future in these countries. When such densities are reached, there will be few alternatives to high-rise living. At that stage, the lessons from Singapore and Hong Kong would have some special relevance.

Transportation

With the expansion of the metropolitan area, the problem of moving people, food, machines and services becomes serious.

Conventional wisdom expected that transportation problems would ease with improvements in communication. When ideas travel by wire, air waves, glass filaments and even laser beams, there might be less need to move people and their things about. Thus a survey of Canadian business travellers elicited the response that about 20 per cent of them would substitute a 'teleconference' device for travel if it were available. Reserach also indicated that about 45 per cent of all business meetings could be substituted by narrow-band devices such as telephone circuits.[28]

Revolutionary developments in communications technology, however, have been slow in easing transportation problems. The traffic jam, more than smoke or smog, has become the real symbol of urban malfunction. The private automobile, although condemned worldwide as an expensive, inefficient, wasteful and polluting menace, shows no signs of departing from the urban scene. Not even the dizzying increase in oil prices since the 1973 oil crisis has stopped the car dead in its tracks.

Prospects for reduction in car numbers are not too bright because a large portion of the world's population has not really enjoyed the pleasures of car ownership yet. In 1976 about 41 per cent of the automobiles in use worldwide were in the United States; another 32 per cent were in Western Europe. The Japanese had 161 automobiles per 1,000 people (about 7 per cent of the world's stock) while the rest of Asia had only three cars per 1,000 people. China, with almost a billion people, had only 37,000 cars. Even the more industrialized USSR had remarkably few automobiles–89 per cent of all travel in the Soviet Union was by train or bus.[29]

The disadvantages of the automobile are well known. The car achieves 16 passenger miles per gallon of fuel on the average, compared to 150 passenger miles for a fully-loaded bus or 400 passenger miles for a high-speed train. The fossil fuel burned in cars causes smog and acid rain. Automobiles need highways, which penetrate wilderness areas and pave over productive crop lands. They also contribute to the development of the polynucleated city, such as Los Angeles and Sao Paulo (in the latter, over half of the city's space is turned over into freeways, roads and parking lots).

With all these disadvantages, it is not surprising that many metropolitan authorities are seeking control of the car. In cities as varied as Tokyo, Toronto, Oslo and Gothenburg, inner-city streets are being closed to cars and transformed into pedestrian malls. Even when cars are allowed in central areas, their movements are severely curtailed. In Gothenburg, Sweden, the central area has been divided into 'cells' in which motorists are allowed to drive freely. However, driving from one cell to another is not allowed; to do this a motorist has to get out through loops and beltways before being allowed to enter another cell. The result of this transport planning has been a steep reduction in inner-city driving and a corresponding increase in the use of public transport.

Much debate now rages in many metropolitan areas between a transport systm based on highways and cars or a public transport system. More and more, voices favouring public transport are being heard. For example, Stockholm's rapid transport system has provided not only efficient service but has contributed to the city's more manageable urban structure. The Bay Area Rapid Transit System in the San Francisco area gives sound competition to the city's fabled cable cars.

The polarized debates between the automobile and public transport, however, are being overtaken by a recent development that reveals the creative genius of urban dwellers faced with a difficult situation. This is the rapid growth of para-transport systems. These systems first originated in cities of less developed countries where the urban poor usually found it difficult to get around, and include *publicos* in Caracas, *peseros* in Mexico City, *jeepneys* in Manila, *dolmus* in Istanbul, *matatus* in Nairobi, *samlors* or *silors* in Bangkok and *betjaks* in Yogyakarta. Para-transports started informally, sometimes illegally – they were spontaneous responses to the transport needs of the people. Basically, they were shared systems: the *dolmus*, for example, is a private car travelling a fixed route. It picks up passengers along the way, who pay when they get off. The systems, however, are flexible: one can hire a *dolmus* like a taxi and pay for its exclusive use. Wherever they are found, governments have found it extremely difficult to regulate para-transport systems. Not surprisingly, most transport authorities have decided to accommodate para-transport into the existing transport systems, making their operations legitimate so that they can be managed better.

Amazingly, the idea of flexible para-transport systems has spread widely to more developed countries where there is increasing dissatisfaction with the car. An Organization of Economic Co-operation and Development (OECD) study identified 485 individual projects in OECD countries that approximate para-transport systems. Among these are dial-a-ride; demand-responsive bus systems; taxi-derived para-transport; collaborative para-transport; and publicars.[30]

In Toronto or Ottawa one can summon a dial-a-ride mini-bus or automobile by telephone. The vehicle is dispatched by a person or a computer that makes sure enough people are going in a specific direction to warrant use of one vehicle. Demand-responsive bus systems use larger vehicles whose scheduling and frequency of trips respond directly to the direction and volume of traffic demand. The taxi-derived system works on the same principle as dial-a-ride but uses special taxi fleets. In Boston, for example, passengers going from the airport to the town can save a lot of money by using the share-a-taxi service.

Collaborative para-transport includes arrangements involving car or van pools as well as volunteer driver schemes. They are the fastest growing types of para-transport because the co-operative efforts of small numbers of people usually result in greater benefits for all. Also growing rapidly are publicar systems, which include self-drive taxis, auto-taxis, or very short-term car rental arrangements. Systems like these provide flexible transport to people living in central cities who can walk or take a bicycle to work but who may need a car for weekend or out-of-town trips.

Although para-transport systems are growing rapidly, the use of the private automobile still shows no sign of slackening. In Japan, for example, the number of cars on the road has increased from a mere one million in 1960 to more than 34 million at present. In Denmark, the use of private cars for trips to central Copenhagen has increased to such an extent that private cars are now involved in 30 per cent of all such journeys. At present, many people in less developed countries ride bicycles, take overcrowded buses or walk. As soon as their earnings reach a certain level, however, they make a trip to the nearest automobile show-room to pick out a car.

The ultimate solution to a metropolitan area's transportation problem calls for a number of complementary measures that would limit the use of automobiles, encourage public transport, improve the efficiency of existing systems, and plan the location of urban activities so that travelling could be minimized. In Singapore, a plan for reducing automobile traffic in the central city has been in operation since 1975: the central parts of the city were turned into 'restricted zones' for cars, and any person wanting to bring a car into this zone during restricted hours now has to pay a licence fee equivalent to $1.50 per day, a steep amount for the average motorist. Because of this expense, downtown traffic in Singapore has been reduced by as much as two-thirds, although essential trips have not been unduly curtailed.

The success of the Singapore plan was based on the provision of ample parking facilities just outside the restricted zone. From these parking lots public buses could be taken to the centre. These buses were allocated special lanes to make them go faster, and the system of traffic lights was also synchronized to make traffic flow more smoothly. Concessional licence fees were provided to residents within the restricted zone as well as to delivery vehicles making essential trips to the area. In this way basic services in the city centre were not adversely affected.

In other metropolitan areas, traffic planners are finding that there are a number of instruments they can use to make transport systems function more efficiently. The simple expedient of painting lanes on much-travelled roads helps to improve traffic flow. Directional lights for specific traffic lanes might be used to control the amount of traffic going in a particular direction. Thus during morning rush hours more lanes could be opened towards the city by directional lights. Lights and signs might also be used to reserve special lanes for buses, para-transports and bicycles or slow-moving vehicles.

Alternative transport modes that do not use much fossil fuel might be encouraged. The bicycle is gaining wide popularity, as are motorized bikes or mopeds. In Dar-es-Salaam government officials are encouraged to travel by bicycle, while in Manila travel lanes reserved for bicycle riders have been proposed.

87 –

Mopeds, which average 135 miles per gallon, are suited to journeys of less than 10 miles. In the United States it has been estimated that 80 per cent of car trips are 10 miles or less, making mopeds more advantageous.

Social Development Services

While housing and transportation grab the attention of metropolitan executives and planners, urban populations usually demand more services related to social development such as health, education, employment and manpower training. Like other urban services, social development needs are directly linked with demographic variables.

In most MDCs, health institutions tend to be formal and structured. A hierarchy of services ranging from the neighbourhood centre to the general hospital exists. Curative medical services are stressed. Professionally trained doctors and nurses staff the institutions. Specialist facilities and expensive medical procedures are favoured.

Unfortunately, this model of a 'modern' health system is increasingly being copied in many less developed countries. The result is that a dualistic gulf develops between the health facilities in capital cities, which cater mainly to urban elites, and those in villages. Because funds for health services are limited they are usually devoted to urban facilities, leading to inadequate and inefficient services elsewhere.

Experiences in a number of countries (China, United Republic of Tanzania, Cuba) show that the health needs of the urban poor can be adequately met by a more informal system. Health volunteers from the community may be trained in the rudiments of health care; they can then be the first line of contact between the health system and the people. In Sri Lanka, for example, the Government recently launched a programme to train 2,606 midwives as basic 'Family Health Workers'. China's 'barefoot doctors' have gained international renown. In Zaïre, traditional healers are being given instruction in modern medicine; so are Philippine *hilots* (traditional midwives) who are trained in family planning and the use of contraceptive devices. In spreading information and disseminating contraceptive aids, in fact, it has been found that basic health workers are excellent channels, especially in urban slum and squatter communities where people still cling to traditional medical beliefs and practices.

The same tendency to borrow MDC institutions in LDCs is found in educational and manpower training systems. Despite the fact that education is usually a joint responsibility between local and national government, metropolitan budgets usually devote the largest portion of resources to it. Among educational expenses, the cost of buildings and teachers' salaries usually comprises more than two-thirds of all expenses. The insistence on formal instruction within the confines of the classroom continues to raise costs, which may, in turn, force local authorities to provide education of a lower standard.

In Indonesia and the Philippines experiments have been conducted on an educational system at the primary level that relies on radio broadcasts and 'learning modules' rather than teachers in classrooms. This experiment, known as Project Impact, uses self-learning instruction booklets that are programmed for easy reading. Lessons covered in the booklets are broadcast at specific times of the day; students listen to the broadcast and apply the contents to their lessons. They may appeal to parents or elder children for help. There are also volunteer workers who assist the teachers in giving personalized instruction. Examinations are given by the teachers at designated centres when the students are ready. There are no regular classrooms and no expensive facilities, and the teacher:student ratio is about 200:1. Educational costs, therefore, have been dramatically reduced, but initial results show that the performance of students trained in Project Impact was equal to, if not better than, that achieved by students enrolled in the more expensive traditional system. These results are currently being assessed to find out if similar levels can be achieved in normal situations that do not benefit from the effects of the experimental situation.

Even in more developed countries, where considerably more resources could be devoted to education, there is some dissatisfaction with traditional approaches. In England and the United States, the post-war baby boom resulted in the construction of expensive school buildings, libraries and gymnasia. Most of these are now used way below capacity as fewer children are being born. The waste is especially acute in more affluent suburban communities with energetic school boards. Ironically, while these suburban facilities are used way below capacity, those in downtown areas serving minority ethnic groups are overcrowded. Differential demographic patterns between recently rural blacks and Hispanics (in the USA) and suburban whites are responsible for these problems. Unfortunately, such means as busing children from one community to another have not been welcomed by people. Relatively little could also be done to correct imbalances in tax resources between inner-city areas and suburbs. In Detroit, Miami, Glasgow and London, area-wide governments are helping to achieve sharing of resources. However, there are still many metropolitan areas where various groups have differential access to educational facilities.

A welcome shift in the educational curricula of many less-developed countries has occurred in the opening up of many vocational schools and national apprenticeship systems. While this trend antedated recent international migration patterns, these two phenomena have tended to feed into each other. Previous international migration has involved either professional and technical migrants to Europe and North America (the so-called brain drain) or the movement of semi-skilled or unskilled workers to Europe. More recently, skilled workers have been attracted to work in the Middle East. Migration to Saudi Arabia, Kuwait, the Libyan Arab Jamahiriya and the United Arab Emirates initially originated from Egypt, Syria, Lebanon and Jordan. By 1970, for example, it was estimated that about 2.5 million workers were involved in these intra-regional exchanges. Lately, workers in affluent Arab states have tended to come from Asia (Pakistan, the Philippines, Sri Lanka and Bangladesh).[31]

Conventional migration theory posits an equilibrium-seeking device wherein labour flows from areas of low incomes to those where incomes are higher. Contemporary migration, however, reveals an ever-widening gap between sending and receiving areas. It is estimated that between 1975 and the year 2000 the global labour force would grow by 900 million people. The vast majority of the new job-seekers would be in countries of low income, where the population is young, birth rates are high, and job markets are overcrowded. Few of these countries would have development plans that stress employment creation, egalitarian income distribution and population stabilization as priorities. With 350 million people in the world already unemployed, these countries show no prospect of helping to alleviate the global situation.[32]

Popular Participation in Urban Management

One of the negative effects of large urban populations undergoing rapid socio-economic changes is personal disorganization and *anomie*. An apartment-dweller in a vast complex or a civil servant in a huge bureaucracy risks suffering from alienation and loss of a sense of efficacy. Faced with onrushing waves of events, the individual might retreat into himself. This feeling of lack of efficacy might lead to cynicism, an uncaring attitude and a loss of a sense of personal worth.

While amalgamation at a higher and larger scale might make metropolitan government more efficient, bigness might make decision-making processes inaccessible to the people. This is the reason why metropolitan governments should provide participatory instruments and forums for individual citizens. In metropolitan Winnipeg, for example, where a unified metropolitan government has been set up, community councils have been organized as vehicles for citizen participation. In Warsaw, Prague and Leningrad, committees at the block or community level plan and manage activities ranging from day-care centres to local elections. *Panchayat* committees in Bombay, *rukum wargas* in Jakarta and *barangay* councils in Manila are examples of local groups that act as participatory channels. In other metropolitan areas participation is achieved through public hearings, media discussions, suggestion boxes and referenda.

It is not only in policy formulation, however, that participation achieves benefits. It is becoming increasingly evident that the service needs of large urban areas cannot be adequately met without the active participation of citizens. In the past, administrative systems that *delivered* services to the people have been the norm. As urban services are stretched to the breaking point, it is becoming obvious that co-operative systems rather than service-delivery systems are needed.

When it snows in Shanghai, people do not wait for bulldozers and trucks to come and haul it away; organized at the block level, they take their shovels and baskets and clear the roads, each family looking after the space in front of its house. Low-income communities in Manila organize *ronda* committees in their areas during the summer months to act as fire-fighting and self-defence units. If a fire breaks out in a slum squatter area, people do not grab their belongings and run–they rush to the scene of the fire and help put it out. The *kampong* dwellers of Surabaya do not wait for the water department to connect piped water to each house–they co-operatively set up artesian wells, water reservoirs and communal lavatories with some support from the Government. Low-cost housing in Havana is constructed with the voluntary labour of *micro-brigadas,* self-contained construction crews composed of masons, carpenters, plumbers, electricians and other skilled people who construct and maintain their communal units. Protective surveillance of street crimes in Hong Kong is effectively carried out with the help of neighbourhood vigilance committees.

In view of the magnitude of services needed in metropolitan areas of the future, co-operative systems such as those mentioned above have a definite role to play in government. Happily, demographic processes are contributing to the establishment of such systems. With rural-urban migration happening at such a rapid pace, most recent migrants are bringing traditional rural-based co-operative systems that have been found successful in such processes as house-building, farm preparation, and harvesting and marketing of crops. Faced with problems of housing, street crime, health and other service shortages in metropolitan areas, recent migrants are falling back on co-operative arrangements that have made rural life viable and productive for them.

This 'rediscovery of the community' in metropolitan planning might seem innovative to some. To sensitive observers of the urban scene, however, the primary group in the midst of city life was never lost. More than two decades ago, Jane Jacobs was extolling the virtues of neighbourliness in a city as impersonal as New York.[33] The need for concerned eyes on the street, the reassuring presence of corner stores and coffee shops, and the civilizing influence of the urban village amidst the concrete canyons and bricks and mortar of the city have not been lost to generations of planners. This sensitivity is now seen in the increased emphasis on renewal programmes that restore and maintain instead of destroy and build. With very rare exceptions the 'federal bulldozer' has been stilled in most cities, and urban planning is now more concerned with people's quality of life than with the physical design and costs of buildings.

There is an interface between governmental functions and community action where service needs of the future have to be provided. With metropolitan governments in both industrialized and less developed countries skirting the margins of bankruptcy and other forms of disaster, there is a need to tap the energies of people. One way of fostering this is by organizing primary group associations at the neighbourhood or block level. These organizations might be arranged hierarchically so that they may serve as interest articulation and mobilizing devices at various levels of the metropolitan structure.

Organizing, motivating and mobilizing community groups might be the main functions of a new type of civil servant at the metropolitan level. In many cities, such civil servants already exist and are known as *animateurs,* (Dakar, Senegal), human settlements workers (Manila), or *promotores* (San Salvador). Rather than attempting to deliver services to the people, these workers try to unlock dormant energies and popular resources to pursue self-help projects. By combining governmental and people's resources, these new workers are able to achieve urban service goals more effectively and efficiently.

Summary and Conclusions

For the foreseeable future, it is evident that rapid rates of population increase responsible for the growth of metropolitan and megalopolitan areas will continue. The twentieth century, which opened with only 2.4 per cent of people living in urban places, will close with more than half of all people in cities. It is true that for the world as a whole, growth rates have been declining since the mid-1970s; however, stabilization of global population is still almost a century away. In the meantime, natural growth rates rather than migrations are becoming more important in city growth. Before zero population growth is achieved, therefore, cities could come to resemble insect colonies rather than human habitats.

One positive development is that urbanization is contributing to the process of demographic transition. The growth of cities is positively correlated with increasing income, improving education, expanding communication channels, enhancing literacy and providing employment and other opportunities for women. Despite many problems cities continue to be the productive centres and the hubs of trade and commerce. They also accelerate social change and contribute to the nation-building process.

Despite environmental degradation, metropolitan governments are showing that sustained and committed efforts can reverse negative tendencies. The citizens of London have 50 per cent more winter sunshine than in 1952 because of the strict implementation of the Clean Air Act. Game fish have been caught again in the Thames; salmon have been caught in Lake Ontario after a massive bi-country campaign between Canada and the United States. The Cuyahoga River, which used to be so polluted with oil that it periodically caught fire, is now cleaned up. The racial riots and other problems of Detroit are now merely bad memories, as the energies typified in the city's Renaissance Center have mobilized common efforts.

There are, of course, no panaceas that will solve metropolitan problems once and for all. A clearer understanding of urban processes, however, especially of the relationships between demographic variables and development factors, would go a long way in formulating metropolitan plans that may help to cope with urban problems of the future. In international efforts to solve problems of metropolitan areas, there are four important issues that have been identified that are worth discussing. These are: area-wide jurisdictions; comprehensive regional planning; metropolitan finance; and co-operative social development

Area-wide jurisdictions. International experience has shown the importance of the 'city-region' in comprehensive planning. A natural region with an urban core, a rapidly urbanizing periphery and rural areas that provide room for expansion is the ideal unit for planning metropolitan development. As observed by Weissman, 'The city-region emerges as the environment in which intensive agriculture, industrial centres, residential communities, cultural and recreational facilities could blend into efficient and pleasing patterns, respecting the individual's, the family's and the community's cycles of daily, periodic and occasional requirements.'[34]

Political inertia and traditions of local autonomy contribute toward political fragmentation that makes management of metropolitan governments most difficult. Increasingly, however, area-wide jurisdictions are being instituted in more-developed and less-developed countries. Within these wider regions, linkages among demographic and socio-economic factors can be more easily established. For example, intra-regional migration patterns can be influenced by transport systems and land-use plans that relate residences to jobs. It may aso be possible to substitute regular commuting for migration, by providing efficient transport networks between city centres and regional hinterlands.

As urban agglomerations grow to the extent that they impinge on the territories of other large urban centres, they result in even larger agglomerations known as megalopolitan areas. Here, again, area-wide action is called for. Such massive agglomerations might be difficult to place under a single political jurisdiction but there is a definite need to plan in a comprehensive manner for the territories affected.

Comprehensive planning. Territorial integration might be achieved by political action or administrative fiat but comprehensive planning is a more complex process that attempts to link demographic, economic, social and political variables by adding to them a spatial dimension. A comprehensive metropolitan plan has been defined as:

(i) A model of an intended future situation covering: specific economic and social conditions; their location; land areas required; and the structures, installations, and landscape that are to provide the physical environment for these activities; and

95 –

(ii) A programme of action and predetermined co-ordination of measures, formulated with a view to achieving the intended situation.[35]

Often, national governments are preoccupied with economic problems to the extent that they fail to integrate physical and socio-economic development plans. Economic targets may be set and the means to achieve them organized without regard for the spatial implications of such action. There are precious few economic policies and programmes that do not somehow have an impact on the distribution of physical elements in space. It is the blind pursuit of these policies and programmes in the past that has contributed to the 'unintended growth' of many metropolitan areas. A comprehensive plan should consider that economic decisions necessarily affect the location of industry, the distribution of population, the patterns of land use and the groups of individuals who would benefit (or pay the cost) of government action. When decisions are made on targets for investment, taxation, employment generation or infrastructure construction, the issues of who are affected by these policies, and where they live within the metropolitan area, should be of the highest priority.

Ideally, comprehensive planning can be most effectively pursued under the aegis of a unified metropolitan government. It is wise to include within a metropolitan jurisdiction such areas as are necessary for an assured water supply for the area, the territory needed for sewage treatment and disposal, the main traffic routes and arteries, industrial and tourism development and the provision of parks and recreation areas. The planning jurisdiction of a metropolitan government, therefore, might extend beyond the actual physical boundaries of the built-up area. This fact need not conflict with territorial jurisdictions of local villages and towns. Authority and power may be shared among the various tiers of local, metropolitan and regional government, so that areas of responsibilities that rationally belong at each level could be vested there. Thus, local units might continue to exercise jurisdiction over local water distribution, garbage collection, police protection, fire and emergency services, etc., while comprehensive planning is lodged at metropolitan or regional levels. Representatives of various levels of government might be included in the governing councils or boards that set policies and plans for the metropolitan planning units.

Metropolitan finance. The issues of area-wide jurisdictions and comprehensive planning logically bring about that of metropolitan finance, because they highlight both the need to raise enough resources over the whole metropolitan area and the need to allocate these resources among the various segments of metropolitan economy and society. Fragmented local governments are financially weak; their amalgamation into some form of area-wide government enables them to raise resources for capital and operating purposes more effectively.

One instrument commonly used for raising metropolitan revenue is the unification of a common tax base and the imposition of a common rate of taxes. There is a tendency among competing local units to attract tax-paying concerns by offering concessional assessments, tax rates and other benefits. A metropolitan-wide tax system avoids this fragmentation and encourages better financial revenue-raising. The real property tax is especially amenable to such area-wide reforms as regional cadastral surveys, the amalgamation of tax rolls, the setting of common assessment rates, the imposition of common tax rates and the management of a larger tax organization, all of which benefit from economies of scale.

A metropolitan approach improves the position of local units *vis-à-vis* the national government. Grants from higher levels of government can best be negotiated when local units are unified. Equalization payments might also be worked out more effectively when local units work in concert; such equalization payments should be considered in relation to central-local relations as well as from the point of view of local-local relations. Within metropolitan regions, the inner city often develops a deteriorating tax base as more well-to-do people flee to the suburbs and poorer people move into the city centre. As a result, the quality of urban services between centre and periphery develops a widening gulf. Area-wide action becomes necessary if this dualism is to be prevented from deteriorating further.

Metropolitan finance is directly affected by demographic

97 –

changes that occur within urban regions. Because migration is directly or indirectly affected by the life cycle, people at different stages in their lives tend to locate in various parts of the metropolitan region. Suburbanites, for example, tend to be young couples with children. They have a larger tax base and can afford to support high levels of urban services such as schools, health facilities and recreation areas and parks. As people become older, they might move to inner-city areas as single-member households or childless couples. At this stage, they tend to have lower incomes and own less taxable property.

Good transport networks tend to encourage commuting, which in turn affects metropolitan finance. Commuters live in the suburbs and pay their income and real property taxes there, although they spend most of their working hours in the city. Some form of area-wide taxation has to be found to correct the inequity. Commuters use the services of the inner city, too, but are not charged for keeping and maintaining them. An area-wide approach may bring about revenue-sharing and equalization payments that spread both burden and benefits to all concerned.

To sum up, metropolitan governments can improve their financial positions by reorganizing toward area-wide jurisdictions. They can raise local revenues better and approach higher levels of government for grants. There are any number of area-wide measures, including taxation, budgeting, auditing and financial controls, that can improve their financial positions. While many of these measures often depend on the powers of central government, area-wide action might improve their bargaining power in attaining parity with such powers. After all, continued metropolitan financial strength is necessary for continued development of the national polity.

Co-operative social development. The most important resource of metropolitan governments, of course, is the citizenry. In providing social services like housing, health, education, transportation and employment, the participation of people is important. This participation is not needed only at the policy formulation stage – it is even more important in the actual execution of policies and programmes.

In less-developed countries, an increasing proportion of people in urban areas are unable to meet the costs of decent housing. Squatting and slum dwelling, therefore, are becoming common, resulting in deterioration of the urban environment. Happily, recent approaches that tap the energies and resources of the people themselves are proving effective in coping with the housing and services problem. By co-operative action, the resources of people and the government are combined and seemingly unsurmountable problems such as lack of services and environmental degradation are controlled, if not actually solved.

The same creative approach being used in housing is being applied to transportation problems. While expensive systems based on automobiles and public transport are set up in more-developed countries, one of the fastest growing transport modes involves para-transport systems that require pooling vehicles, sharing rides and splitting the costs of transport. It is significant that para-transport systems originated in less-developed countries and are now increasingly being adopted in more industrialized ones. With the energy crisis, the increasing threats of environmental pollution and the increasing costs of transport systems, the more efficient use of technology in moving people and things around is to be welcomed.

In the past, the development of large cities has depended quite heavily on technological innovations. As more and more cities pass the million mark, it is becoming obvious that technology is not sufficient to keep them producing and to maintain a wholesome environment at the same time. Since people are a city's most important resource, some forms of co-operative management are needed. A shift has to occur from a simple service-delivery system to a more participatory and co-operative management system. This shift calls not only for new governmental structures and procedures but for a new type of civil servant as well. Such a civil servant should be an expert in encouraging and motivating citizens to help in keeping and maintaining urban services. Citizens' resources and energies have to be tapped and organized to keep the cities of the future functioning effectively.

Notes

1. J. C. Russell, 'Late Ancient and Medieval Population', *Transactions of the American Philosophical Society,* XLVIII (June 1958): 63–68. Also Hugh Thomas, *A History of the World* (New York: Harper and Row, 1979), p. 226.

2. United Nations, *Trends and Prospects in the Population of Urban Agglomerations, 1950–2000, as Assessed in 1973–75* (New York: UN, 1975).

3. United Nations, *Urban and City Population 1950–2000 in the World; More Developed and Less Developed Countries* (New York: UN, 1979), Annex A and B. See also *Age-Sex Distribution in Rural and Urban Areas,* (New York: UN, 1979).

4. Richard Meier, 'Relations of Technology to the Design of Very Large Cities', in *India's Urban Future,* ed Roy Turner (Berkeley: University of California Press, 1962), pp. 312–23.

5. Rafael M. Salas, speech delivered before the 34th Session of the United Nations General Assembly, 31 October 1979.

6. George Grier, 'Population Dynamics, Housing Economics and the Future of the American Habitat', in *The Many Facets of Human Settlements, Science and Society,* ed Irene Tinker and Mayra Buvinic (Oxford: Pergamon Press, 19), p. 144.

7. Luther Gulick, *The Metropolitan Problem and American Ideas,* (New York: Alfred A. Knopf, 1962), p. 36.

8. Frank Smallwood, *Greater London, the Politics of Metropolitan Reform* (New York: Bobbs-Merrill Co., Inc., 1965).

9. Philip M. Hauser and Robert W. Gardner, 'Urban Future: Trends and Prospect', paper presented at the UNFPA Conference on Population and the Urban Future, Rome, 1–4 September 1980 (Section 3 of the present book).

10. Aprodicio A. Laquian, *Rural-Urban Migrants and Metropolitan Development* (Toronto: Intermet, 1971). See also Sally Findley, *Planning for Internal Migration: A Review of Issues and Policies in Developing Countries* (Washington, DC: US Bureau of the Census, 1977).

11. John F. C. Turner, 'Uncontrolled Urban Settlement: Problems and Policies', paper presented at the Inter-regional Seminar on Development Policies and Planning in Relation to Urbanization, Pittsburgh, 1966.

12. R. E. Parke and E. W. Burgess, *The City* (Chicago: University of Chicago Press, 1925).

13. Thomas L. Adcock, 'Painting the Town Red', *Passages,* April 1980, p. 34.

14. Raymond Vernon, *Metropolis 1985,* (New York: Doubleday, 1963).

15. Population Reference Bureau, *Population Handbook* (Washington, DC, 1978), p. 41.

16. United Nations, *Administrative Aspects of Urbanization* (New York: Public Administration Division, 1970). Doc. No. ST/TAO/M/51.

17. Government of India, *Report of the Rural-Urban Relationship Committee,* Vol. 1 (New Delhi: Ministry of Health and Family Planning, 1966), pp. 18–23.

18. Ursula Hicks, 'Financing Metropolitan Government', in *Metropoli-*

ﻟ ﻟ ﻟ ﻟ

tan Problems, International Perspectives, ed Simon Miles (Toronto: Methuen Publications, 1970), p. 367.

19. Ann-Marie Walsh, *The Urban Challenge to Government* (New York: Frederick A. Praeger, Inc., 1969).

20. Tokue Shibata, 'Notes on Municipal Finance', paper presented to the UN Workshop on Administrative Aspects of Urbanization, The Hague, 11–20 November 1968.

21. Ursula Hicks, 'Economic and Financial Problems of Metropolitan Areas', *Zeitschrift für Nationalökonomie,* 1969, p. 12.

22. World Bank, *Housing Sector Policy Paper* (Washington, DC: World Bank, 1975). See also T. R. Lakshmanan, L. Chatterjee, and P. Roy, 'Housing Requirements and National Resources: Implications of the UN World Model', in *The Many Facets of Human Settlements,* ed Tinker and Buvinic, p. 283.

23. Marga Institute, *Housing in Sri Lanka* (Colombo: Marga Institute, 1976).

24. Alberto Harth Deneke, 'The Housing Programme of the Fundación Salvadorena de Desarrollo y Vivienda Minima', (PhD dissertation, Department of Urban and Regional Planning, Massachusetts Institute of Technology, 1978).

25. Anthony Churchill, *et al.,* 'Basic Needs in Shelter', (mineograph, World Bank, Washington, D.C., 1978) See also A. A. Laquian, 'Whither Sites and Services', *Science* 192, No. 4243 (1976): 950–55.

26. Stephen H. K. Yeh, *Housing in Singapore, a Multidisciplinary Study* (Singapore: University of Singapore Press, 1975).

27. Luke S. K. Wong, *Housing in Hong Kong* (Hong Kong: Heinemann Educational Books (Asia) Ltd, 1979).

28. Richard C. Harkness, 'Selected Results from a Technology Assessment of Telecommunication-Transportation Interactions', Proceedings of the International Electrical Engineers Conference, Philadelphia, June 1976.

29. Lester E. Brown *et al., Twenty-Two Dimensions of the Population Problem* (Washington, DC: Worldwatch Paper No. 5, 1976), p. 18.

30. Organization for Economic Co-operation and Development, *Para-Transit in the Developing World: Neglected Options for Mobility and Employment* (Paris: OECD Development Centre, 1977), Vols I and II.

31. United Nations, *Trends and Characteristics of International Migration Since 1950* (New York: UN, 1979, Doc. No. ST/ESA/SER.A/64), p. 50.

32. Kathleen Newland, *International Migration: the Search for Work* (Washington, DC: Worldwatch Paper No. 33, 1979), p. 8.

33. Jane Jacobs, *The Death and Life of Great American Cities* (New York: Vintage Books, 1961).

34. Ernest Weissmann, 'Planning and Development of the Metropolitan Environment', in *Metropolitan Problems,* ed Miles, pp. 411–50.

35. United Nations, *Planning of Metropolitan Areas and New Towns* (New York: UN, 1967, Doc. No. ST/SOA/65), p. 37.

Lincoln Christian College

–3–

National and Regional Issues
and Policies in Facing the
Challenges of the Urban Future

SALAH EL-SHAKHS
Rutgers University

*Assisted by Thomas Clark, James Hughes, Meera Kosambi,
Ronald Parker, Ramon Sevilla, and Richard Tomlinson*

Introduction

This background paper provides a general framework for discussing trends and policies that are likely to have a major impact on the future of large urban areas. Such an assessment should help identify the basic areas of challenge to national and regional population and development strategies and clarify the options for response to such challenges.

National policy requirements of large cities can be expected to vary significantly with the nature of the predominant spatial development trends (polarization or deconcentration) at the inter-regional and intra-regional levels. The appropriateness of these policies will also be conditioned by each country's spatial, economic and political context, and its position within the international economic system. While there is a danger of oversimplification in attempting to evaluate and to make prescriptions for the urban policies of so broad a range of countries as are present at this Conference, the wealth of information on wide-ranging experiences possessed by the participants should enable us to avoid that danger.

Relevance of National Policy

The pressures, demands and challenges facing urban governments, particularly in the largest cities, and their capacity to respond to them are in large part determined by national and international forces beyond their scope or influence. There are a number of reasons for this:

(i) The challenges and tasks facing large cities defy traditional political and administrative boundaries and arrangements.[1] International interactions, which directly and indirectly affect large cities, are related to policies of national governments. Similarly, implicit and explicit national policies and regulations of development, integration and communications underlie the functional and structural changes in the urban system and set in motion powerful forces that affect its long-range trends.

(ii) Local governments often lack adequate power and resources to effect major changes within their own boundaries. In a large number of countries, municipal authorities are delegations of the national government's power and depend on national decisions for the major part of their financing, organization and operations.[2] In several countries the largest cities, particularly capital cities, are under the direct control of national governments.[3]

(iii) On the other hand, large urban centres exert powerful influences far beyond their boundaries. Their impact on the development of the rest of the urban system, on rural areas, on regional balance, on the diffusion of social and technical innovations and, generally, on the nature of national economic and social integration and welfare, are legitimate concerns of national governments.

(iv) In most countries, national policies and decisions related to urbanization and urban development are still largely scattered throughout various ministries and agencies. Concern with integrated national urbanization strategies is a recent phenomenon. Few countries have created specialized national agencies to co-ordinate such policies and strategies, and even that co-ordinating effort poses several operational and administrative issues.[4]

As a result, there is limited experience with integrated explicit urbanization strategies. National governments, however, cannot afford the luxury of inaction or of trial and error methods in influencing urbanization and spatial transformations. By the very nature of their functions, governments are already shaping the outcome of such processes in a number of ways that directly or indirectly affect large cities. Thus national governments hold a unique dual responsibility for the future of large urban centres. By their plans, policies and decisions (or lack of them) they influence the emergence of the problems with which urban centres must cope, on the one hand, and have a direct impact on the capacity, efficiency and output of urban governments on the other.[5]

National Policy Contexts

The nature and degree of impact of national policy on the development of urban systems vary considerably with the country's developmental context, its predominant orientation and its capacity to initiate and implement integrated urbanization policies and strategies. In assessing their relevance and effectiveness, therefore, one has to start by a distinction in terms of the country's planning orientation and style.[6] In this regard, a distinction should be made between countries with market or mixed economies and those that are centrally planned and controlled. In the former, market forces are allowed to influence the spatial system to varying degrees, through greater freedom of movement of population and factors of production. Government policies in this context, by and large, are 'adaptive' and attempt to manipulate the processes of urban and spatial development primarily through strategic interventions. In the second group, government policies tend to be 'normative' and to guide the development processes through greater control.[7]

Beyond this, there are a number of factors that would influence the classification of countries for purposes of evaluating trends and policies. These include: spatial contexts (size, physical constraints, spatial distribution of natural resources, present settlement network, regionalization), demographic characteristics (level of urbanization, heterogenity of the population, dynamics of population growth), and economic development (resource base, level of development, participation in the international economy).[8]

The range of developmental factors, differences in their intensities, and the variation in their relative importance and interactions make any broad classification scheme unsatisfactory. Yet such classification is necessary if one is to assess the relevance of wide-ranging experiences and evaluate significant trends and policy implications as a broad guide to individualized country-specific policy formulation efforts. It is with such objectives and limitations in mind that countries can be classified in terms of:

(i) *Structural relationships within the system.* The degree of spatial, social and economic integration within the system would range from relatively independent regional systems through strongly unified dependent national systems to highly interdependent subsystems. This classification would be based on the extent of regionalization (spatial/population size, physical constraints, population diversity, density and distribution, regional identity, cultural historical roots, resource distribution and regional links with the rest of the world).

(ii) *Level of development and resource base.* Countries would be classified as high, medium and low in terms of their economic development characteristics. These include the level of economic development, extent and diversity of natural resources, capacity of local markets, labour force and employment (formal-informal), patterns of ownership, income distribution, and role and participation in the international economy.

While clarifying such developmental contexts would help identify policy options, and their likely impacts on the future of all cities, policy choices are necessarily determined in terms of national goals and priorities and the country's institutional and economic capacity to implement them. History has shown, however, that there is a strong circular interaction between societal conditions, goals and policies. In fact characteristics and conditions of large cities themselves often help determine national goals and policies that affect their own future. Thus evaluation of alternative policy and strategy options is in effect also a process of clarification of national goals and priorities.

National Urban Policy Areas

If there is but one common characteristic among all of the largest cities in the world, it has to be their increasing sensitivity to, and dependence on, national government policies across a wide range of political, social and economic activities. Such policies can be categorized as having a direct or an indirect impact on large cities. This paper focuses primarily on national policies in influencing large cities as entities within urban systems.

Further, these policies, whether implicit or explicit, will be analyzed within a spatial development framework, in other words the dynamics of spatial reorganization of population and activities. Such policy areas are indirect: national population and economic growth and development, population distribution relative to resources and economic opportunities, and the structure of the national urban settlement hierarchy; and direct: core region (including large city) growth or decline, development of core region settlement subsystem, and urban redevelopment and efficiency of the large city. A later section discusses most policies, instruments and strategies relevant to each of these areas and the ways in which they would influence the future of large cities. The appropriate choices of policy mix and strategies, as will be discussed later, will depend on the individual context, and their timing should be placed within a long-range perspective.

The Need for a Comprehensive Long-range Perspective

An effective framework for national urban policies requires their integration in terms of economic and social development objectives, sectoral and spatial impacts, and short-term and long-range implications. Such integration, however, implies a high degree of clarity, articulation and commitment on the part of policy-makers, economic planners and physical (spatial) development specialists involved in the development process.

Social and political objectives promulgated by spatial development strategies are frequently in conflict with the forces created by national economic policies. Thus, while efficiency-oriented economic plans tend to be spatially biased, spatial development strategies tend to underestimate the power of economic linkages and psycho-social forces, or to ignore their own economic and institutional limitations.[9] Integrating economic and spatial development plans, therefore, requires a better understanding of their consequences and limitations and of the trade-offs involved.

Policies designed to correct an imbalance within the system frequently serve instead to intensify that very imbalance or, in the long run, to create new demands that are more difficult or costly to satisfy.[10] Paradoxically, programmes intended to speed the spread effects from core regions, in less developed countries (LDCs), and to develop the hinterlands sufficiently to entice their populations to stay there often result in increasing migration to the core. Similarly, restrictive policies and punitive measures ('closed city' programmes), aside from their practical limitations and moral implications, may set in motion processes of ageing, obsolescence and inefficiency which result in long-range structural imbalances and problems in large cities.

Inadequate knowledge of the dynamics of spatial development processes severely limits the ability to predict their long-range patterns with reasonably accuracy and the capacity and certainty of shaping them through public policy. This is particularly true in rapidly changing LDCs with market and mixed economies.

Spatial development patterns in any system are sensitive to uncertain technological and political developments from both within and without. Furthermore, they are characterized by major time-lags and may be discontinuous over the long range, and therefore improperly judged by their short-term trends and outcomes.[11] Urbanization policies based on uncertain long-range predictions could become restrictive rather than adaptive and prove to be costly in the long run.

While most LDCs may have to cope, over the coming generation, with the urban explosion, it is clear that the corner on the population explosion of a generation ago 'has been turned much faster than anyone predicted'. Fertility rates have begun to decline in several LDCs, faster than they did in the more developed countries (MDCs).[12] In several MDCs, despite comparative qualifications, the turnabout in the growth of large metropolitan areas should be instructive. The United States and several Organization of Economic Co-operation and Development (OCED) countries, who as recently as the 1960s were preparing for anticipated growth in their large metropolitan areas, are now busy trying to cope with the emerging decline of these areas. Indications are that several middle-income countries may soon be approaching a similar process of polarization reversal.

An understanding of the forces of spatial polarization and of polarization reversal, and the timing and conditions under which they occur, has enormous implications for our ability to predict future urban challenges and to design appropriate, flexible, long-range strategies to face them. Such strategies may require hard political choices that many governments are either unwilling to make or unable to address. Because of the rapid rate of change and the pressures it brings about, governments tend to spend most of their efforts coping with these and have little time, resources and energy left to look far ahead or to co-ordinate their efforts.

Spatial Development Trends

Recent interest in urban change and development has been prompted by the seemingly close interaction between the processes of economic development and of urbanization, and the accompanying functional and spatial shifts of population and economic activities.[13] Understandably, such shifts have increasingly become a concern of public policy, in both LDCs and MDCs, because of their implications for national economic growth, equitable distribution of development benefits, national integration and the future of large metropolitan cores.

The nature and magnitude of such shifts, and their consequences for large cities, depend on the stage and condition of economic development in individual geographic areas. The size and spatial distribution of urban population are influenced by a number of complex processes that are not yet fully understood and are susceptible to forces that are not easily predicted. Thus while one may be reasonably confident of predictions concerning long-range changes in total population and the proportion of that population defined as urban, the ability to predict the future size and form of very large cities is much more suspect.

The future of these cities should be assessed within a long-range spatial development framework. Related theory must cope with a wide range of relevant variables as well as with diverse geographical and cultural contexts.[14] Further, it has frequently been argued that the historical and current experience of the MDCs is of little relevance to the future of the LDCs because of major differences in their internal developmental contexts and their respective roles in the international system.[15] Recent experiences in some LDCs, however, seem to indicate that, despite differences in cultural and developmental contexts, there may be more to learn from each other's experiences than has been suspected. Altough the forms and rates of the processes of urbanization and counter-urbanization may vary, their causes and the forces influencing their outcome may be very similar. Understanding such long-range trends and the forces behind them is essential if meaningful policies are to be established.

Comparative Analysis of 33 Urban Systems

The world's major cities play a significant, and sometimes dominant, role within their respective nations. National policy regarding these cities can have a substantial impact on national economic performance, as well as on the pattern and magnitude of welfare disparities among sub-national regions. The following analysis considers such linkages, focusing on the 60 world cities (urban agglomerations) whose populations are expected to exceed five million by the year 2000, and the 33 nations in which they exist. It covers current conditions, developmental trends over the last three decades, and empirical evidence of the relationship among the national urban system, regional inequality and national economic performance.

Urban concentration-deconcentration trends. The cities and nations included in this analysis, on the basis of their participation in this conference, do cover a wide geographic, developmen-

–110

tal and size spectrum. A simple size and development level classification (Table 3.1) suggests that the cities that claim the larger shares of their respective national urban populations tend to be located in the smaller nations. Consequently, large cities tend to be more dominant in smaller nations, while larger nations, often with larger territories, tend to develop several rival centres.

In most world regions major urban agglomerations have become increasingly dominant over the last third of a century. From 1950 to 1980, the populations of the majority of these cities in Africa, Latin America, East Asia and South Asia have grown far more rapidly than their respective national populations. Only in North America and Europe did the population dominance of the majority of cities decrease (Table 3.2).

In fact a recent study of migration to and from broadly defined core regions of 18 countries shows that either a reversal or a severe decline in the level of net population flow into such regions occurred in 11 of the 18 at various times during the last 20 years. These included France and the Federal Republic of Germany (in the 1960s) and Italy and Japan (in the 1970s).[16] In fact, other data indicate that many metropolitan areas in the United States and Western Europe were declining in both relative and absolute terms by the 1970s. These include New York, Detroit, Los Angeles and Paris, which is estimated to have lost 300,000 people between 1968 and 1975.

With a few exceptions, increasing large city dominance, with GDP growth, is characteristic of the less developed world regions. Among high-income nations, however, primacy declines with *per capita* GDP. This suggests the notion of polarization reversal at higher levels of development, that is, primacy tends to increase in the early stages of development and tends to decrease at higher levels (i.e. an inverted U curve of primacy on development). For policy purposes, however, a distinction should be made between urban concentration within a city system (primacy) and the existence of very large cities in that system, since the two phenomena do not necessarily coincide.[17] This is particularly the case in very large countries and those with distinct regions or city sub-systems such as India, China and Nigeria of

Table 3.1. *Large Cities Classified According to National Per Capita Gross Domestic Product (1976) and Size of Nation (1980).* (City as Percentage of Urban Population 1980).

Total National Population, 1980	Per Capita National Gross Domestic Product (US $, 1976)				
	Under 300	301–500	501–1400	1401–3500	Over 3500
Under 15 Million			*Chile* Santiago (36.0)	*Hong Kong* Hong Kong (100.0)	
			Iraq Baghdad (53.0)	*Venezuela* Caracas (26.0)	
15–50 Million	*Burma* Rangoon[1] (35.0)	*Egypt* Cairo[1] (39.0) Alexandria[1] (13.0)	*Columbia* Bogota (22.0)	*Argentina* Buenos Aires[1] (47.0)	
	Vietnam Ho Chi Minh City (26.0) Hanoi (20.0)	*Morocco* Casablanca (27.0)	*Peru* Lima–Callao[1] (49.0)	*Iran* Teheran (32.0)	
	Zaire Kinshasa (35.0)	*Thailand* Bangkok–Thonburi[1] (48.0)	*Republic of Korea* Seoul (47.0) Pusan[1] (15.0)	*Spain* Madrid (15.0)	
			Turkey Istanbul[1] (19.0) Ankara (11.0)		

51–100 Million

Bangladesh
- Dacca[1] (32.0)

Pakistan
- Karachi[1] (24.0)
- Lahore (12.0)
- Faisalabad (8.0)

Nigeria
- Lagos (20.0)

Philippines
- Manila[1] (28.0)

Mexico
- Mexico City (30.0)
- Guadalajara (6.0)

Italy
- Milan (17.0)
- Rome (9.0)

Federal Republic of Germany
- Rhein–Ruhr (19.0)

France
- Paris (23.0)

United Kingdom
- London[1] (25.0)

Over 100 Million

China[2]
- Shanghai[1] (5.0)
- Beijing (4.0)
- Tienjin[1] (2.0)
- Wuhan (1.0)
- Lanzhou (1.0)
- Baotou (1.0)

India
- Calcutta[1] (6.0)
- Bombay[1] (5.0)
- Delhi (4.0)
- Madras[1] (3.0)
- Bangalore (2.0)
- Ahmedabad (2.0)

Indonesia
- Jakarta[1] (22.0)
- Surabaja[1] (7.0)

Brazil
- Sao Paulo (16.0)
- Rio de Janeiro[1] (12.0)
- Belo Horizonte (3.0)

Soviet Union
- Moscow (16.0)
- Leningrad[1] (12.0)
- (3.0)

Japan
- Tokyo–Yokohama[1] (5.0)
- Osaka–Kobe[1] (3.0)

United States
- New York[1] (10.0)
- Los Angeles (6.0)
- Chicago (4.0)
- Philadelphia[1] (3.0)
- Detroit (3.0)

[1] Coastal location.

[2] China's *per capita* gross domestic product has been estimated by the author in the absence of published information.

GENERAL NOTES: All city population data corresponds to urban agglomerations identified by the major city within them. With the exception of Rome, all these cities are expected to have a population equal to or in excess of 5 million by the year 2000.

Table 3.2. Populations of the 60 Urban Agglomerations Expected to Have Over 5 Million Persons in the Year 2000, in 1950, 1980 and 2000 (Projected)

City (Country)	Population (Millions)			City's Population In 1980 As a Percentage of:	
	1950	1980	2000	National Population	Total Urban Population
Africa					
Alexandria (Egypt)	0.9	2.9	5.6	6.9	13.0
Cairo (Egypt)	2.4	8.4	16.4	20.0	39.0
Casablanca (Morocco)	0.6	2.3	5.2	11.3	27.0
Lagos (Nigeria)	0.3	2.9	9.4	4.0	20.0
Kinshasa (Zaire)	0.2	3.0	9.1	10.7	35.0
Latin America					
Buenos Aires (Argentina)	4.5	10.4	14.0	38.4	47.0
Belo Horizonte (Brazil)	0.4	2.6	5.7	2.1	3.0
Rio De Janeiro (Brazil)	2.9	10.0	19.4	7.9	12.0
Sao Paulo (Brazil)	2.5	12.5	26.0	9.9	16.0
Santiago (Chile)	1.3	3.5	5.1	31.3	36.0
Bogotá (Colombia)	0.7	4.4	9.5	14.6	22.0
Mexico City (Mexico)	2.9	13.9	31.6	19.9	30.0
Guadalajara (Mexico)	0.4	2.6	6.2	3.7	6.0
Lima–Callao (Peru)	0.6	5.2	12.1	29.4	49.0
Caracas (Venezuela)	0.7	3.2	6.0	22.7	26.0
North America					
Chicago (USA)	4.9	7.5	9.3	3.3	4.0
Detroit (USA)	2.8	4.5	5.7	2.0	3.0
Los Angeles (USA)	4.0	10.7	14.8	4.8	6.8
New York (USA)	12.3	17.9	22.2	8.0	10.0
Philadelphia (USA)	2.9	4.5	5.6	2.0	3.0
East Asia					
Shanghai (China)	5.8	12.0	19.2	1.3	5.0
Beijing (China)	2.2	10.2	19.1	1.1	4.0
Tienjin (China)	2.4	4.7	7.5	0.5	2.0
Wuhan (China)	1.1	3.4	5.8	0.4	1.0
Lanzhou (China)	0.3	2.4	5.1	0.3	1.0
Baotou (China)	—	2.0	5.3	0.2	1.0
Hong Kong (Hong Kong)	1.6	4.3	5.5	96.0	100.0

Tokyo–Yokohama (Japan)	6.7	19.7	26.1	16.7	21.0
Osaka-Kobe (Japan)	3.8	9.7	12.6	8.2	11.0
Seoul (Republic of Korea)	1.0	9.4	18.7	25.1	27.0
Pusan (Republic of Korea)	0.5	2.9	5.1	7.8	15.0
South Asia					
Dacca (Bangladesh)	0.4	2.1	5.9	2.0	32.0
Rangoon (Burma)	0.7	3.1	7.4	8.8	35.0
Calcutta (India)	4.4	9.6	19.7	1.4	6.0
Bombay (India)	2.9	8.7	19.1	1.3	5.0
Delhi (India)	1.4	5.7	13.2	0.8	4.0
Madras (India)	1.4	4.7	10.4	0.7	3.0
Bangalore (India)	0.8	2.5	5.4	0.4	2.0
Ahmedabad (India)	0.9	2.5	5.5	0.4	2.0
Jakarta (Indonesia)	1.6	7.2	16.9	4.6	22.0
Surabaja (Indonesia)	0.7	2.3	5.0	1.5	7.0
Teheran (Iran)	1.0	5.8	13.8	15.1	32.0
Baghdad (Iraq)	0.6	4.6	10.9	35.1	53.0
Karachi (Pakistan)	1.0	6.0	15.9	7.2	24.0
Lahore (Pakistan)	0.8	3.1	7.7	3.7	12.0
Faisalabad (Pakistan)	0.2	2.0	6.2	2.4	8.0
Manila (Philippines)	1.5	5.6	12.7	10.7	28.0
Bangkok-Thonburi (Thailand)	1.0	4.3	11.0	8.7	48.0
Ankara (Turkey)	0.3	2.3	5.3	5.1	11.0
Istanbul (Turkey)	1.0	4.0	8.3	8.9	19.0
Hanoi (Vietnam)	0.2	1.9	5.1	3.9	20.0
Ho Chi Minh City (Vietnam)	1.0	2.4	5.1	4.9	26.0
Europe					
Rhein-Ruhr (Federal Republic of Germany)	6.8	9.9	11.3	16.0	19.0
Paris (France)	5.4	9.9	12.3	18.0	23.0
Rome (Italy)	1.7	3.5	4.6	6.2	9.2
Milan (Italy)	3.6	6.5	8.3	11.5	17.0
Madrid (Spain)	1.6	4.1	5.9	11.0	15.0
Moscow (USSR)	4.8	8.2	10.6	3.1	5.0
Leningrad (USSR)	2.6	4.6	6.1	1.7	3.0
London (United Kingdom)	10.2	11.0	12.7	19.0	25.0

SOURCE: United Nations, Department of Economic and Social Affairs, Population Division, 'Trends and Prospects in the Populations of Urban Agglomerations, 1980–2000, As Assessed in 1973–1974, (ESA/P/WP 58) 21 November 1975, Table C.

Table 3.3 Current Selected Characteristics of the 33 Nations Expected to Have at Least One City Having a Population of More than 51 Million by the Year 2000

Region and Nation	Population 1980 (Millions)		Growth Rate 1950–80 (Per cent)		Population of Largest City as percentage of: (1976)		Gross Domestic Product 1976 (US $)		Income Inequality Index	
	Total	In Cities[1] Over 100,000	Total	In Cities Over 100,000	Population In Next Three Largest Cities[2]	Total Population	Total (Billions)	Per Capita	Regional[3] (1976)	National[4]
Africa										
Egypt	42.1	13.0	105	210	164	11.1	14.9	349		.434
Morocco	20.4	4.9	127	250	126	9.7	8.1	453		
Nigeria	72.6	5.1	137	292	63	1.2	28.8	445		
Zaire	28.0	1.9	146	533	405	3.4	3.7	146		
North America										
USA	224.1	130.7	48	96	198	7.8	1,701.7	7,911	.134[5]	.407
Latin America										
Argentina	27.1	16.5	58	312	155	39.0	47.4	1,844	.313	.411
Brazil	126.4	42.8	143	370	81	7.7	144.7	1,325	1.620	.647
Chile	11.2	4.1	84	356	482	27.4	11.3	1,075		.376
Colombia	30.2	11.7	167	485	109	11.8	14.8	608	.307	.562
Mexico	70.0	23.8	171	386	263	17.8	79.1	1,270	.534	.583
Peru	17.7	4.2	113	367	338	18.4	13.4	840		.594
Venezuela	14.1	5.1	176	410	123	20.2	31.1	2,510	.533	.477
East Asia										
China	907.6	130.7	62	222	76	1.1	9.2	2,099		.430
Hong Kong	4.5	4.5	125	181		100.0			.301	.287
Japan	117.5	66.2	41	198	152	11.9	555.2	4,922		.372
Republic of Korea	37.4	12.1	82	290	154	14.6	25.4	707	.308	
Southeast Asia										
Burma	35.2	2.4	87	140	188	4.4	3.5	113		.381
Indonesia	154.9	18.7	104	307	134	3.8	37.3	267		.463
Philippines	52.2	8.3	157	232	75	10.7	17.8	407		.466
Thailand	49.5	3.9	153	225	271	5.8	16.3	379	.678	.448
Viet Nam	48.6	3.3	116	154	163	4.4	7.6	156		

Southwest Asia

Iran	38.5	8.8	136	283	234	11.5	66.8	1,988	.923	.502
Iraq	13.1	4.0	152	400	199	14.3	15.7	1,363		.629
Turkey	45.4	8.4	118	394	98	7.4	41.1	999		.568

South Central Asia

Bangladesh	92.5		232				7.9	85		
India	694.3	69.4	96	144	67	1.4	86.0	141	.185	.477
Pakistan	83.0	8.5	235	130	97	2.8	14.5	200		.330

Europe

Federal Republic of Germany	62.0	33.6	22	37	74	11.0	445.8	7,249	.135	.394
France	55.1	23.5	32	116	128	16.9	346.6	6,552	.243	.518
Italy	56.3	16.6	20	75	69	5.4	170.8	3,040	.272	
Poland	35.3	10.9	41	88	70	7.3	98.2	2,856		.264
Spain	37.2	12.4	33	85	113	9.1	104.7	2,908		.393
USSR	268.1	84.2	49	125	97	2.9	708.2	2,759		
United Kingdom	57.5	41.2	14	13	264	20.5	219.2	3,922	.109	.339

[1] Population in cities having more than 100,000 persons. Estimated by applying the proportion of the total population residing in this city class in 1970 to the 1980 estimate of total population.

[2] This is the four-city index of first-city primacy. It is the ratio of the population of the largest city to that of the next three largest.

[3] The regional inequality index is the coefficient of variation. This is the ratio of the standard deviation of regional per capita incomes (weighted according to the relative population size of regions) to the mean regional *per capita* income. The index is directly related to the level of inequality among regions, decreasing to a minimum value of zero as total equality is achieved.

[4] This is the Gini coefficient. It is directly related to the level of inequality, falling to zero as total aggregate national equality is achieved. For this sample of 33 nations, the Gini, Kuznets and entropy coefficients of aggregate income inequality are highly correlated. All the Gini coefficients pertain to years since 1960, except in the case of Burma (1958), and Iraq (1956). See the original source for the type of income data used in each instance.

[5] The United States coefficient is unweighted; calculated by the author.

Table 3.4. Correlations[1] Among Current National Characteristics: Cross-Sectional Analysis

(Correlation coefficients, with the numbers of nations in parenthesis)

	Population (1970)[2]			Primacy 1970 — Largest City as Percentage of:		Gross Domestic Product (1976)		Inequality	
	National Total	In Cities Over 100,000	Largest City	(A) Total Urban Population[3]	(B) Three Next-Largest Cities	Total	Per Capita	Regional[4]	National[5]
National Population	1.00								
Population in Cities	.75 (33)	1.00							
Largest City Population	.39 (33)	.78 (33)	1.00						
Primacy (A)	-.43 (33)	-.44 (33)	-.14 (33)	1.00					
Primacy (B)	-.34 (30)	-.32 (30)	.02 (30)	.80 (30)	1.00				
GDP: Total	-.24 (12)	.92 (33)	.73 (31)	-.35 (31)	-.21 (29)	1.00			
GDP: Per Capita	.07 (31)	.63 (31)	.66 (31)	-.23 (31)	-.11 (29)	.76 (31)	1.00		
Inequality: Regional	-.15 (14)	-.22 (14)	-.22 (14)	.02 (14)	-.08 (13)	-.27 (14)	-.36 (14)	1.00	
Inequality: National	-.04 (26)	-.20 (26)	-.19 (26)	.06 (26)	.23 (24)	-.20 (26)	-.26 (26)	.64 (13)	1.00

[1]Row and column headings are identical in this matrix of Pearson correlation coefficients. The higher the absolute value of the coefficient, the stronger the relationship between any two variables. The sign of the coefficient indicates the direction of the relationship, whether positive or negative. Note that both inequality indices decrease absolutely as equality increases. Due to missing data, the number of cases (nations) for which each coefficient is calculated will vary.

[2]City populations correspond to the populations of urbanized areas wherever such data were available. City-proper (political definition) data are used whenever data for urbanized areas were not available. Growth rates of cities may be understated when city-proper rather than urbanized area data are employed, though not necessarily.

[3]The size threshold above which settlements are considered urban varies among nations.

[4]The regional inequality index is the coefficient of variation, applied to regional incomes weighted according to relative regional populations. It decreases as income equality among subnational regions increases. The index is sensitive to the number of subnational regions. The year for which the index has been estimated is not the same for all nations.

[5]The national inequality index is the Gini coefficient. It decreases as equality among income intervals increases. These intervals vary among nations.

the LDCs, and Italy, the United States and the Soviet Union of the MDCs. The analysis indicates a moderate negative relationship between primacy and national population (Tables 3.3 and 3.4); that is, as national population increases, the degree of primacy will diminish as rival urban centres and regions develop outside the core area in which the largest city exists.

The analysis of the 33 nations also confirms the strong relationship between the level of urbanization (in cities with over 100,000 population) and total national prosperity GDP, and a positive relationship, though not as strong, with *per capita* GDP. In general, the total (GDP) has been growing faster than populations in these countries. Smaller nations seem to have higher growth rates of both national population and of the degree of primacy of the largest city.

Regional inequality, national economic performance and the urban system. Changes in regional income inequality with development have generally been found to behave in a pattern similar to that of changes in the degree of urban concentration.[18] Both tend to increase during the early stages of development in LDCs and decrease in later stages of development in MDCs. Of course there are exceptions to this general pattern. In the analysis of the 33 nations in general, and a subset of nations for which regional income data are available (Table 3.5, Parts B and C), these consistent exceptions include: India, Nigeria, Brazil and the Republic of Korea (of the LDCs), and France and Japan (of the MDCs). The patterns of development in these countries are subjected to individual analysis below.

In general, however, the analysis indicates that countries with higher GDPs exhibit higher levels of regional equality. This positive correlation between national prosperity and greater equality among sub-national regions is strongest in the case of MDCs. In the LDCs, a negative correlation between *per capita* GDP and regional equality exists (i.e. higher income is associated with higher inequality) and is particularly strengthened by the cases of Brazil, Iran and Venezuela. There also exists a strong positive correlation between regional and aggregate national inequality (Table 3.3).

119 –

Polarization Reversal in Selected Countries

Several countries representing major world regions and different development levels and sizes (area and population) have been selected for further consideration (Table 3.6). All these countries experienced a significant increase in both the absolute population

Table 3.5. Cross Tabulations of Selected Countries According to Urban Primacy[1], Regional Inequality[2] and National GDP Per Capita[3]

PART A
Urban Primacy
and GDP Per
Capita

		National GDP Per Capita	
		Over $2750	Under $2750
	High Dominance Over 20 per cent	France Japan Poland United Kingdom	Argentina Colombia Egypt Iraq Mexico Morocco Peru Philippines Republic of Korea Thailand Venezuela
URBAN PRIMACY	Low Dominance Under 20 per cent	Federal Republic of Germany Italy Spain USA USSR	Brazil India Nigeria

PART B
GDP Per Capita
and Regional
Inequality

		Regional Inequality	
		High Inequality (Index Over .44)	Low Inequality (Index Under .44)
	High Over $2750		Federal Republic of Germany France Italy Japan United Kingdom United States
GDP Per Capita	Low Under $2750	Brazil Iraq Mexico Thailand Venezuela	Argentina Colombia India Republic of Korea

PART C Urban Primacy and Regional Inequality		*Regional Inequality*	
		High Inequality (Index Over .44)	Low Inequality (Index Under .44)
	High Dominance *Over 20 per cent* URBAN PRIMACY	Iraq Mexico Thailand Venezuela	Argentina Colombia France Japan Republic of Korea United Kingdom
	Low Dominance *Under 20 per cent*	Brazil	Federal Republic of Germany Italy United States

[1]The measure of urban primacy used here is the population of the largest city as a percentage of the urban population in 1980.

[2]The regional inequality index employed here is the coefficient of variation, weighted according to the relative size (population) of subnational regions. It is a measure of *per capita* income accounting procedures of individual nations, and to the number and configuration of subnational regions in single nations.

[3]'GDP' is the gross domestic product in 1976 US $.

and the share of national population residing in cities having over one million persons during 1950–70 (except Nigeria which had no cities in this size class). In six countries (the United States, Mexico, Brazil, France, Poland and the Soviet Union) the rate of increase in the share of national population in these cities was higher during 1960–70 than in the previous decade (Table 3.7). This rate was higher during 1950–60 than 1960–70 for seven countries (Egypt, the Republic of Korea, Japan, the Philippines, India, Italy and Spain), a trend which may signal the beginning of deconcentration.

Medium-sized cities in the half-to-one-million-sized group gained substantial proportionate growth at the expense of all other-size classes in Brazil, the United States and the Soviet Union during the 1950s, and in the Republic of Korea, Japan and Poland in the 1960s (Table 3.7). In the case of Nigeria, the two half-million-sized cities, Lagos and Ibadan, also gained substantial growth in the 1960s, but they are the two largest Nigerian cities. Regional centres in the 100,000–500,000 category registered substantial proportionate gains during the 1960s in Mexico and Egypt. However, this may not necessarily indicate the beginning of deconcentration because of shifts of cities among size classes.

121 –

Table 3.6. Urban-economic Profiles of 18 Countries

Nations in Rank Order of Per Capita GDP 1976	POPULATION				PRIMACY		NATIONAL PRODUCT		RESOURCE DISTRIBUTION	
	1980 (Millions) in Cities		Growth Rate 1950–80 (Per cent)		Population of Largest City as Percentage of: (1976)		Gross Domestic Product 1976 (US Dollars)		Income-Inequality Index	
	Total	100,000 and over	Total	Cities[1] 100,000 and over	Population in Next Three Largest Cities[3]	1980 Urban Population	(Billions) Total	Per Capita	Regional[3] (1976)	National[4]
Least Developed										
1. India	694	69	96	144	67	6.0	86	141	.185	.477
2. Egypt	42	13	105	210	164	39.0	15	394	—	.434
3. Philippines	52	8	157	232	75	28.0	18	407	—	.466
4. Nigeria	73	5	137	292	63	20.0	29	445	—	—
5. Morocco	20	5	127	250	126	27.0	8	453	—	—
Lower-Moderate										
6. Colombia	39	12	167	485	109	22.0	15	608	.307	.562
7. Republic of Korea	37	12	82	290	154	47.0	25	707	.308	.372
8. Peru	18	4	113	367	338	49.0	13	840	—	.594
9. Mexico	70	24	171	386	263	30.0	79	1,270	.534	.563
10. Brazil	126	43	143	370	81	16.0	145	1,325	1.620	.647
Upper-Moderate										
11. Venezuela	14	5	176	410	123	27.0	31	2,510	.533	.477
12. USSR	268	84	49	125	97	23.0	708	2,759	—	—
13. Poland	35	11	41	88	70	15.0	98	2,856	—	.264
14. Spain	37	12	33	85	113	17.0	105	2,908	.272	.393
15. Italy	56	17	20	75	69	17.0	171	3,040	—	—
Most Developed										
16. Japan	118	66	41	198	152	21.0	555	4,922	.301	.287
17. France	55	24	32	116	128	23.0	347	6,552	.243	.518
18. United States	224	131	48	96	198	10.0	1,702	7,911	.134	.407

[1] Population in cities having more than 100,000 persons. Estimated by applying the proportion of the total population residing in this city class in 1970 to the 1980 estimate of total population.

[2] This is the four-city index of first-city primacy. It is the ratio of the population of the largest city to that of the next three largest.

[3] The regional inequality index is the coefficient of variation. This is the ratio of the standard deviation of regional *per capita* incomes (weighted according to the relative population size of regions) to the mean regional *per capita* income. The index is directly related to the level of inequality among regions, decreasing to a minimum value of zero as total equality is achieved.

[4] This is the Gini coefficient. It is directly related to the level of national inequality, falling to zero as total aggregate national equality is achieved. For this sample, the Gini, Kuznets and entropy coefficients of aggregate income inequality are highly correlated. All the Gini coefficients pertain to years since 1960.

Table 3.7. Population Deconcentrations: Growth Rates of Percentage[1] of National Population in Four City-size Classes, 18 Nations, 1950–60 and 1960–70[2]

(Percentages) City-size Classes[3]

Region and Nation	1950–60				1960–70			
	100,000	100,000–499,999	500,000–1 Million	Over 1 Million	100,000	100,000–499,999	500,000–1 Million	Over 1 Million
Africa								
Egypt	5	71	—	17	9	33	—	14
Morocco	40	23	15	—	12	4	−58	—
Nigeria	30	−5	—	—	22	12	100	—
North America								
USA	−3	4	39	15	−13	0	−12	31
Latin America								
Brazil	5	25	208	38	1	−6	−5	61
Colombia	12	3	−30	—	−25	15	95	110
Mexico	2	5	—	28	0	55	−71	42
Peru	7	—	0	—	−13	317	—	33
Venezuela	33	79	0	—	19	−20	—	19
Asia								
India	−2	17	−22	14	−1	0	86	10
Japan	100	70	−10	56	25	32	68	33
Philippines	−3	16	—	14	0	23	—	7
Republic of Korea	68	6	4	100	27	12	148	35
Europe								
France	−2	65	17	11	−8	32	−43	34
Italy	0	11	−6	54	−7	20	−15	41
Poland	33	32	−3	8	18	35	77	44
Spain	5	8	−6	28	−3	22	−12	22
USSR	17	12	37	15	23	27	1	59

[1] For example, in 1950, 7.3 per cent of Morocco's total national population resided in cities having fewer than 100,000 population. By 1960 this figure had risen to 10.2 per cent. This table shows the growth rate of this percentage, which in this case would be 40 per cent.

[2] Blanks indicate that the share of national population at the start of the time interval was zero.

[3] As cities grow or decline they may shift from one size class to another.

As mentioned above, the United States, France, Italy and Japan are already experiencing a process of deconcentration within their urban systems. Within metropolitan areas, central cities experienced such trends of reversal or decline much earlier and to a greater degree. Of the areas represented at this Conference, at least five central cities (Philadelphia, Chicago, Detroit, Paris and London) lost population in the 1960s and three (New York, Los Angeles and Tokyo) in the 1970s.

Patterns of concentrations. The Nigerian spatial system has undergone a long process of integration, from pre-colonial autonomous systems to three semi-autonomous and ethnically diverse regions and, after independence, into a consolidated federal hierarchy. At the apex of this hierarchy stood metropolitan Lagos. Lagos grew at four times the rate of national population growth, and it acquired most of the industrial and modern service activities in the nation at the expense of traditional regional centres like Sokoto, Kano and Ibadan. Both physical (transport) and political integration played a critical role in the growth of Lagos from a small city of 50,000 around the turn of the century into a metropolis of over three million today.[19]

Although Lagos is not yet a gigantic metropolis, by world measures, it was less prepared and less suited for such rapid growth than most. Furthermore, Nigeria's relatively low level and rapid rate of urbanization likely will increase the pressures on Lagos despite the presence of two secondary core regions in the country and the efforts to build a new capital.[20]

India's urban settlement system is characterized by strong regionalization, or multiplicity of sub-systems, with wide variations in regional urban growth rates and high degrees of primacy (urban concentration) within regions. Thus while India has very large cities and high rural-urban disparity, its national system as a whole shows relatively low degrees of concentration. Such balanced inter-regional distribution of urban growth is due to a number of factors: sheer distances as well as geographic and population size and diversity (relative regional independence), historical development of port cities and administrative centres and, unlike Brazil or Nigeria, a relatively low level of regional income inequality (approaching that of the United States, despite low levels of urbanization and economic development).

India's medium-sized cities (100,000–500,000 class) have been growing relatively fast, as a group, further reflecting and reinforcing the regionalization of the urban system. While unbalanced intra-regional concentration or metropolitanization continues, recent evidence indicates that a process of intra-metropolitan deconcentration shifts are occurring at least in Bombay and Delhi.[21]

Extreme regional inequalities characterize the Brazilian development process and the urban settlement system. Increasing concentration of economic power and of industrial activities between 1920 and 1968 focused on the Sao Paulo region, to the detriment of the underdeveloped northeast. The traditional centralization of power and protectionist policies of manufacturing effectively discouraged agriculture and regionalization of development, thereby increasing spatial growth disparities and aggregate national income inequality despite rapid rates of national economic growth.[22] Income and urban concentration and dualism evident at the national (inter-regional) level are also evident at the regional level, where large metropolises are expanding their boundaries and influence into vast urban fields.[23]

Analysis of experience in the Republic of Korea indicates that while net migration to the Seoul metropolitan area is still high, the rate of population concentration has now passed its peak and is declining, largely due to declining income disparities among regions.[24] At the regional level, the degree of urban concentration has declined in both the mid-western and south-western regions since 1970. These trends accompanied rapid economic and urban growth. In addition, the small size of the country, geographic features related to an export orientation, and government pricing policies may all have contributed to the early reduction in income disparities and the beginnings of urban deconcentration.[25]

Patterns of deconcentration and dispersal. Paris dominated the French city system far more, and much longer, than similar cities in other developed countries. Its dominance and growth

SALAH EL-SHAKHS

accelerated with relatively rapid population and economic growth in the post-World War II period. The shift from agriculture to industry focused on the Paris region up to 1962.[26]

Such dominance, however, has recently been declining, at least in terms of relative population growth. There has been a net outflow of native population from the Paris region to the rest of France, particularly the relatively underdeveloped western part, since 1968. This, however, was compensated by international migration. But by the early 1970s the positive net migration to the region had been reversed.[27] Thus after a long history of centralization and urban population concentration, France has begun a process of inter-regional deconcentration. Shifts in manufacturing employment seemd to favour the regions closest to Paris, however, and the decline in secondary employment in the region since 1962 was more than compensated for by the tertiary sector.[28]

The cities that benefited early (between 1954 and 1962) from this concentration process were those in the 100,000 and 200,000 population categories. While isolated rural municipalities lost population, those within commuting range from cities continued to grow.[29] Within the Paris region itself, the periphery continued to grow while the centre city lost population between 1960 and 1975.

The Japanese experience in concentration and deconcentration focused on its core region is generally not dissimilar to that of France. Japan witnessed major population shifts from the peripheral islands and non-metropolitan areas to the Tokaido urban region during a period of rapid economic growth and industrialization prior to 1970. Reverse shifts in population and economic activities first favoured suburban areas, then close-by medium-sized centres and finally medium-sized cities in the periphery. These shifts were strongly related to income differentials and to tertiary activities.[30] Thus recently there has been a decline in net population flows into the core region, a U-turn migration of the rural young back to cities near home, a decline in the rate of growth in suburbs of major cities, and a rapid growth of medium- and small-sized cities. These shifts seem to have continued in the 1970s to the extent that Tokyo and Osaka are now experiencing absolute decline.[31]

Nowhere else have the processes of urban deconcentration

- *126*

Table 3.8. Population Change for Selected Group of Metropolitan and Non-metropolitan Counties in the United States: 1960, 1970 and 1977

AVERAGE ANNUAL PERCENTAGE CHANGE

Metropolitan areas, non-metropolitan counties and regions	Population		Natural Increase		Net Migration	
	1970 to 1977	1960 to 1970	1970 to 1977	1960 to 1970	1970 to 1977	1960 to 1970
United States	0.9	1.3	0.7	1.1	0.2	0.2
Metropolitan	0.7	1.6	0.7	1.1	0.1	0.5
Over 3,000,000	0.1	1.4	0.6	1.0	-0.5	0.4
1,000,000 to 2,999,999	0.9	1.9	0.7	1.2	0.3	0.8
500,000 to 999,999	0.9	1.5	0.7	1.2	0.2	0.4
250,000 to 499,999	1.3	1.4	0.8	1.2	0.5	0.2
Less than 250,000	1.4	1.5	0.8	1.2	0.6	0.3
Non-metropolitan counties by commuting to metropolitan areas	1.2	0.4	0.6	0.9	0.6	-0.6
20 per cent or more	1.7	0.9	0.5	0.8	1.2	0.1
10 to 19 per cent	1.2	0.7	0.5	0.8	0.7	-0.2
3 to 9 per cent	1.1	0.5	0.6	0.9	0.5	-0.4
Less than 3 per cent	1.1	0.1	0.6	1.0	0.5	-0.9
North-east	0.1	0.9	0.4	0.9	-0.3	0.1
Metropolitan	-0.1	1.0	0.4	0.9	-0.5	0.1
Non-metropolitan	1.2	0.8	0.4	0.8	0.8	—
North Central	0.3	0.9	0.6	1.0	-0.3	-0.1
Metropolitan	0.2	1.2	0.7	1.2	-0.5	0.1
Non-metropolitan	0.6	0.2	0.4	0.8	0.2	-0.6
South	1.5	1.3	0.8	1.2	0.7	0.2
Metropolitan	1.6	2.0	0.8	1.3	0.8	0.8
Non-metropolitan	1.2	0.3	0.6	1.0	0.6	-0.8
West	1.6	2.2	0.9	1.3	0.8	1.0
Metropolitan	1.5	2.5	0.8	1.3	0.7	1.3
Non-metropolitan	2.4	0.9	1.0	1.2	1.5	-0.4

SOURCE: US Bureau of the Census, *Current Population Reports*, Series P-20, No. 336, 'Population Profile of the United States, 1978,' (Washington, DC: USGPO, 1979).

and dispersion, under market conditions, been as pronounced as in the United States. The American urban experience through 1980 can be capsulized into three distinct phases: the rise of the central city (from 1860 to 1910); the emergence of metropolitan areas (from 1910 to 1960, with suburbanization as a dominant thrust during this period); and, with the 1960s, the beginnings of the third phase of urban evolution, setting the stage for population spillover and the beginnings of broader regional shifts. During the 1970s, suburbanization was joined by an accelerating inter-regional shift, metropolitan non-metropolitan growth reversals and expanding intra-metropolitan differentials–all taking place within a nation whose rate of population increase has substantially diminished over the past two decades (Table 3.8).

With this slow growth context, the south and west regions captured the bulk of absolute population gains since 1970, while the older core regions in the northeast and north central states are experiencing growing rates of net out-migration. The 1970s also marked the end of a long-term trend of metropolitan growth, the annual rate of which fell from 1.6 per cent in the 1960s to 0.7 per cent. It is the largest metropolitan areas (over 3 million) that are at the forefront of this slowdown, while smaller metropolitan areas and non-metropolitan areas are gaining. Within metropolitan areas, the 1970-77 period marked the first time that the nation's central cities as a group experienced absolute population losses (4.6 per cent), with those in the largest metropolitan areas accounting for the majority of the losses.

These patterns of inter-regional and intra-regional shifts have been attributed to a large number of complex forces and processes. They include technological and economic development, the distribution of political power among the states, decreasing regional income inequalities, integration and homogenization of space and of national markets and the increasing physical, organizational and technological hardening and obsolescence of older cores.[32]

The resulting process of counter-urbanization has thus replaced urbanization 'as the dominant force shaping the nation's settlement pattern'.[33] It points to nothing less than a state of total urbanization characterized by highly interdependent and integrated networks of small specialized urban settlements arranged within vast dispersed urban regions.[34]

– 128

Settlement Systems and Spatial Development

The process of population dispersal and urban implosion and homogenization in the United States may indeed be too unique, in terms of its tempo, form and underlying causes, to serve as a model for things to come in other countries and cultures, yet it may well serve as a warning. As the preceding analysis seems to indicate, the forces and sequence of concentration-deconcentration processes in urban systems at both regional and national levels provide an essential framework for assessing the short-term and long-range trends of the urban future.

The basic differences are those of timing, intensity and form. Spatial deconcentration of urban population is either emerging or has already occurred in countries both with (Sweden, France, Poland) and without (the United States, Japan, Republic of Korea) strong urban decentralization policies.[35] Similarly, the concentration of population in large metropolitan areas and the subsequent expansion of their urban fields and the formation of urban regions is taking place in many countries with or without specific urban policies.

Underlying long-range trends in urban systems. Although definitive universal patterns of changes in spatial and size distribution of urban settlement systems are somewhat elusive, partly because of the major historical and spatial differences among countries and partly because of the tremendous influences of international interactions among city systems,[36] a general pattern of change in the size distribution of urban settlements within systems of cities during the process of national development is being confirmed with the passage of time [37]

This pattern points to a process in which urban functions and population tend toward spatial concentration during the early stages of development in one or a few favoured core areas within national systems. Such tendencies towards polarization become stronger the more they reinforce the favourable position and comparative political and economic advantage of these cores. This process continues, however, until regional income and development disparities begin to decline through a process of diffusion of political and economic power and reduction in the relative comparative advantage of the core.

Thus the concentration process will continue up to a point at which either:

(i) the increasing social awareness of the nation and developments in its social and political system no longer tolerate the ever increasing disparities; or

(ii) it becomes economically more profitable for investments to spread into the less developed areas and resources; or

(iii) a combination of both.

Only after this turning-point (polarization reversal) does the development process move in the direction of reducing disparities and inequalities among regions and within the urban settlement system.[38]

Regions within national spatial systems will tend to follow a similar pattern, in which the most-developed region (core area) is likely to be the first to undergo a process of intra-regional deconcentration (or dispersion) followed by other regions as they reach appropriate concentration and economic and social development thresholds. In fact deconcentration within the core region would probably precede and signal the beginning of polarization reversal (Figure 3.1). This distinction, however, would not apply in small countries whose spatial system essentially consists of one region or even a metropolitan area (e.g. Singapore, Hong Kong and several Caribbean nations).

While such a long-range perspective on ultimate changes within the urban system is useful both as a general guide and as a target for long-range planning, it provides few practical clues for the interim design of public policy. The timing and concentration thresholds of polarization reversal, the form of the resulting size and spatial hierarchy, and the optimality of such distributions can vary considerably with the spatial, economic and political development contexts of countries.[39]

The divergence in experiences is closely related to differences in the initial conditions and relative distribution within the system, economic and political structure, and the nature of the processes of international and national integration.

Types of urban settelement systems. The size and spatial structure of most existing urban settlement patterns can be described in terms of four general types which reflect the basic economic conditions and extent of integration within the system.[40] This typology is intended as both a classification of initial conditions and a convenient way of positioning countries with

Figure 3.1. Patterns of Change in Primacy with Development, and in Regional
Inequalities with National Integration

(a)　　　Primacy

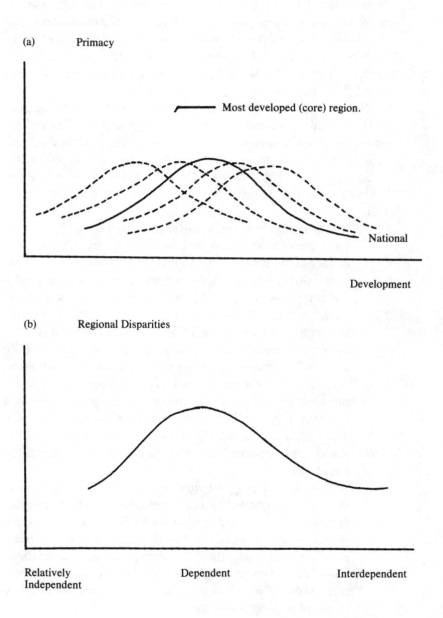

Development

(b)　　　Regional Disparities

Relatively　　　　　　　Dependent　　　　　　Interdependent
Independent

SPATIAL INTEGRATION

respect to the long-range spatial development trends described earlier, using these trends as a basis for policy evaluation and formulation. Of course these types are intended to highlight the dominant features and processes at work in different systems and at different levels of development, and will not fit all countries or be expected neatly to fit a specific country. In fact, as indicated earlier, different regions, particularly in large countries, may fall into different types.

Moreover, these four types do not cover the two extreme ends of the spatial development spectrum, i.e. the pre-urban unintegrated rural settlement systems or future patterns of total urbanization. Neither of these extremes seem to exist in the world today, and thus countries would tend to fall into one of the following four types, as indicated by the sample (Table 3.9, Figure 3.2).

*Type I: Relatively independent regional networks:*These systems are characterized by low levels of urbanization and of income and relatively high rates of population and urban growth. Primary activities and agriculture are predominant. Most cities function primarily as local and regional central places in a more evenly distributed urban hierarchy with low levels of inter-regional inequality.

Type II: Integrated dependent primate hierarchies: These systems are characterized by moderate levels of urbanization and of income and relatively high population growth rates but very high urban growth rates. Agriculture is still dominant, but with moderate levels of industrialization. The urban system would show very high degrees of national concentration and urban-rural and inter-regional inequalities.

Type III: Interdependent metropolitan subsystems: These systems are relatively more developed, with high levels of urbanization, income and industrialization. They have relatively low population and urban growth rates, more evenly distributed urban population in more specialized and well-connected metropolitan and regional centres, high levels of physical and economic integration and low levels of regional inequality.

Type IV: Highly integrated interdependent urban regions:

Table 3.9. Selected Country Profiles or Urban Hierarchy Groups

	Per Capita GDP 1976 US$	Urban Population (in percentages) 1980	Average Annual Urban Growth Rate 1970-5	Largest City as Percentage of Urban Population 1980	Average Annual Population Growth Rate 1970-6	1976 Population Density Per Sq Km	Per cent Ratio of Population Dependent on Agriculture to Rural Population 1976
Type I:							
India	141	23	3.6	6	2.1	186	90
China	—	25	4.3	6	1.7	89	92
Nigeria	445	20	4.6	20	2.7	70	86
Morocco	453	38	5.4	27	3.0	40	90
Type II:							
Egypt	349	51	4.2	39	2.2	38	94
Philippines	407	38	4.2	28	2.9	146	106
Republic of Korea	707	53	6.6	47	—	—	85
Mexico	1,270	63	4.8	30	3.5	32	108
Brazil	1,325	63	4.7	16	2.8	13	96
Iraq	1,363	66	4.9	50	3.4	27	88
Type III:							
Spain	2,908	72	1.8	15	1.1	71	96
USSR	2,759	64	2.3	5	0.9	12	83
Italy	3,040	69	1.2	17	0.8	187	50
Japan	4,922	78	2.3	21	1.3	303	58
France	6,552	78	1.6	23	0.7	97	58
Type IV:							
Federal Republic of Germany	7,249	85	0.7	19	0.3	155	38
USA	7,911	76	1.4	10	0.7	23	21

SALAH EL-SHAKHS

Figure 3.2. Types and Spatial Evolution of Urban Settlement Systems
(Generalized Patterns)

Type I:
Relatively Independent
Regional Networks

Type II:
Integrated Dependent
Primate Hierarchies

Type III:
Interdependent
Metropolitan Subsystems

Type IV:
Highly Integrated
Interdependent
Urban Regions

These systems have very high levels of urbanization and
of income and extremely low levels of population and urban growth. They are highly industrialized, with a very
small proportion of the labour force in agriculture and a
substantial portion in tertiary activities. The urban system
would be characterized by an interlocking system of urban
fields with a high degree of specialization, intensity of interaction, inter-urban mobility and inter-regional equality.
The key variables among these types are the level of development and the nature and extent of integration (and their
impact on spatial inequalities). In this sense, several sub-types
would take into account factors influencing these two variables,

– 134

e.g. size, diversity, resource base and distribution, and political system.

System Integration and Regional Disparities

High degrees of concentration in urban systems (primacy) appear to be an inevitable consequence of the cycle of political and economic polarization-dependence characteristic of the early stages of development under market conditions. This cycle is usually reinforced by unfavourable conditions in integration within the international economic system and the unequal basis of political and economic integration within national spatial systems which tend to increase inter-regional disparities (Figure 3.1b) The latter is not only associated with increased population concentration in core regions, but indeed often credited with causing them. There is some evidence that well-intentioned efforts of spatial and economic integration, such as expanding transportation networks and decentralizing modern industries, when designed to reduce inequalities or concentration or both at early stages of development, tend to produce opposite results and increase rather than reduce such inequalities.

These integration efforts are based on neo-classical assumptions about flows of labour and capital, and assumptions that innovations, and therefore development and income, will diffuse down the urban hierarchy and spread out of urban centres into their hinterlands. Instead, however, at early stages of development and low levels of urbanization, they generally tend to unleash powerful polarization forces (backwash effects). Such forces overpower embryonic hierarchical settlement patterns, focus the attention and aspirations on the national core region, and enforce national urban concentration and primacy, particularly in small countries where space does not present major accessibility barriers.[41]

Thus increased economic integration and spatial interaction among units (countries or regions) with widely disparate levels of development will initially tend to reinforce and increase disparities and dependencies to the disadvantage of the less developed units. This will permit flows of labour and capital to move beyond the boundaries of local regions, increase the

135 –

knowledge and experience of potential migrants, and strengthen their perceptions of disparities, thus leading to greater migration flows.[42]

An exception to this process may exist if the local markets of the less developed regions were protected by their relative isolation until they developed sufficient scale economies (in terms of population and income) to generate or attract industries that cannot serve them from the core region. This may have been the case in the experience of the MDCs.[43] Also, relative isolation may explain the low levels of national primacy and inequalities in very large countries where long distances, the large size of regional sub-systems and strong regional identity act as barriers against strong national spatial and functional accessibility. Such systems would tend to develop strong intra-regional concentration and primacy patterns focused on large regional centres (e.g. India and China).

Other exceptions to the pattern of increasing disparities with integration, in the early stages of development, may exist as a result of strong measures of redistribution, including dispersed political power, strong controls of both flows and means of exchange, and/or specialized resource endowments that favour the less developed areas.

As countries reach higher levels of development, they seem to develop a strong negative relationship between national prosperity and regional inequality: i.e. higher levels of national prosperity signify greater equality among sub-national regions. Greater integration at those levels would tend to speed the process of regional equality and thus increase national aggregate equality as well, since the analysis indicates a strong positive relationship between the two.

These patterns imply an eventual reversal in the relationship between the extent of national integration and regional disparities and sustained national economic growth. Indeed declines in regional disparities in development levels and urban concentration have largely been attributed to autonomous changes and development within their national economies, rather than to the effects of public policy.[44] This does not necessarily imply, however, that disparities could not be reduced through public policy; rather that the policies may not have been appropriate, or may have been applied at the wrong time, within their economic and political contexts.

The eventual reversal of polarization trends seems to be contingent on achieving an equitable social and spatial distribution of development benefits and of political power. Such redistribution, however, could entail high economic costs under conditions of underdevelopment, and/or high political costs under conditions of ethnic and spatial diversity. On the other hand, unmitigated polarization processes could lead to similar costs, particularly in the long run.

Future Urban Challenges

The future urban challenges thus lie primarily in the economic and political systems' ability, at both the international and national levels, simultaneously to expand the economy and equitably distribute its resources–'growth with distribution', in an effort to moderate the impacts of expected spatial transformations while dealing with contemporary socio-economic issues.[45]

As the foregoing analysis seems to imply, the urban future is one of long-range convergence in patterns (equi-finality of systems) despite different initial conditions and divergent paths.[46] It suggests that processes and problems of concentration inter-regionally (centered on core regions) and intra-regionally (focused in central cities) would eventually give way to the reverse processes and problems of deconcentration and dispersion, respectively. Such reversal is predicated on continued economic growth and developments in transportation and technology, innovation diffusion, shifts in locational preferences and a similar reversal pattern in the rates of national population growth. The ultimate result is the 'total urbanization' of spatial systems in the form of vast interdependent 'urban fields' or urban regions. Ultimately, within a country's spatial context, such patterns will lead to:

(i) an expansion in the number of urban settlements or the establishment of new settlements;

(ii) an expansion of the boundaries, influence and urbanized land area of urban settlements;

(iii) transformation of large cities into large metropolitan complexes or urban regions and complexity of spatial flows and interactions;

(iv) increased spatial shifts of, and aggregate demand for, non-agricultural employment in secondary and tertiary activities.

This expansion and this spatial shift within the national urban system, whether they are those of concentration or deconcentration, tend to be characterized at any given point in time by a number of lags in the process of urban development and imbalances in its outcome. They underlie the challenges to national urban policy and underscore the problems of urban government. These are primarily:[47]

(i) the lags in the process of adjustment between: the rate of expansion and shifts in the urban system, and the commitment and capacity for planning; changes in the scope and complexity of urban functions, and adaptations in administrative and political institutions and boundaries; changes in the economic system, and spatial and social response;

(ii) imbalances between: population distribution and the distribution of resources and of employment opportunities; the cost of services and of urban land, and the ability of both individuals (particularly the poor) and municipalities (particularly large cities) to pay for them; responsibilities and tasks facing local governments, and the authority and capacity to handle them.

Challenges of Concentration (LDCs)

Countries undergoing the process of urban concentration (Type I and II countries) are faced with the challenges of promoting national economic growth and full utilization of their resources, yet at the same time promoting regional equity and avoiding or reducing excessive development disparities and concentration. While these two objectives may not necessarily be in conflict with each other, particularly within a long-range development perspective, they require co-ordinated economic and spatial development policies and plans, at both regional and national levels, for the efficient distribution of population and economic activities.[48]

The policy challenge. The challenge to such planning efforts lies in their ability to:

(i) anticipate future spatial structures and, in the process of attempting to solve current problems, lay down the basis (in terms of both physical and institutional infrastructure) for their eventual emergence;

(ii) hasten the process of spatial transition and moderate the rates and impacts of extreme spatial shifts (first of concentration and later of deconcentration);

(iii) provide flexible and timely responses to the emergence of signs of change and avoid reinforcing the status quo and current trends.

Policy issues. There are a number of policy issues related to this effort:

(i) Population distribution: the need to rationalize population-resource relationships focuses the attention on issues of population distribution (within rural and rural-urban areas) and inequalities. These include the impact on: population growth, economic expansion, social development, political stability and the performance and efficiency of the urban system. Population distribution patterns and objectives change with development and are influenced not only by the nature and distribution of natural resources but also by the orientation of the economy, structure of land ownership and production and distribution relationships.[49]

(ii) Rural-to-urban migration: the ability to control or modify the rate, direction and characteristics of migration flows is crucial because of their impacts on the areas of origin and of destination, on the migrants themselves, and generally on the rates of national population and economic growth.[50] Guiding migration, particularly during the early stages of development when it is not perceived as a major issue, would help establish the future structure of the urban system and development of large cities during subsequent stages of rapid urbanization. The determinants and impacts of migration, however, change with development. Its proper guidance requires not only economic and technical resources but also responsible and flexible administrative and political institutions.

(iii) The urban hierarchy: cities have been described as the engines of development; their size and spatial distribution determine their efficiency in performing such a role. Suggestions have frequently been made for a balanced urban hierarchy in line with central place precepts. This means a large spatially organized pattern of towns and cities of all sizes with numbers decreasing as sizes and functions increase. Such a pattern, it is argued, would help create a wider range of options for migrants, vitalize rural areas through easy access to services and amenities, counteract the attraction of primate cities through competitive regional centres, serve the needs of urban industrial growth through the development of sufficiently large-scale economies in intermediate-sized cities, and help diffuse innovation and growth impulses down the urban hierarchy.

Counter-arguments, however, have maintained that such hierarchies fail to spread innovations and income effects positively, may encourage greater migration from rural areas, may spread available resources too thin to have an impact, and may reduce the overall economic growth potential of concentrated urbanization.

The optimality of urban distributions is a function of the spatial context and the levels of urbanization and of development. There is no magic formula for an optimum urban distribution since it changes over time. While a more balanced urban hierarchy would help smooth spatial transitions, and ultimately enhance the efficiency of the future urban system, its efficiency at any given point in time is a function of the society's goals (with respect to inter-regional equity for example) and the performance of its largest urban centres.[51] Thus the size of urban distribution focuses on the minimum efficient size of cities.

(iii) The size and efficiency of cities: studies of the optimum size of cities seem to point out that while a minimum-size threshold may indeed be necessary to achieve adequate economies of scale, within a country's context, an optimum size (at which the net benefits of additional growth becomes zero) is much more questionable. The former is a function of the location and role of the city and the development of its urban system, while the latter is a function of internal organization and planning

– 140

capacity.[52] Optimality thus becomes a more subjective concept related to level of development and development goals, capacity to plan and culturally determined tolerance levels of interaction. Thus the notion of minimum size may indeed require high degrees of primacy at low levels of urbanization and development.[53] However, the arguments that continued urban concentration beyond that point may be necessary for overall national economic efficiency or that cities will become less efficient beyond a certain size become meaningless. If the rapid growth of the largest city is not associated with, or necessary for, major additional industrial expansion within the system and if the capacity to organize, plan and service very large cities is low (which is the case in most LDCs), then pursuing hierarchical balance and distributional equities become the significant challenges for both short- and long-range policies.

(iv) Planning orientation: characteristically, most development efforts and international assistance in countries with relatively low levels of urbanization go into building up their basic spatial, economic and social infrastructure. This results, directly or indirectly, in 'space forming' projects that will influence the rate and direction of their future urbanization. It also underscores the urgent need for long-range comprehensive spatial development plans.

The dilemma facing many of these countries (e.g. African nations), however, is that such plans normally require extensive data and professional resource inputs that they do not have, and capital resources and time that they can ill afford. Planning efforts have to compete for scarce resources with badly needed, immediate and tangible development projects. Thus they are given lower priority and end with meagre allocations, if any at all.[54]

The low level of commitment and the weak state of comprehensive planning at the national, regional and metropolitan levels generally result in lack of co-ordination, policy conflicts, and inability to take account of either system-wide consequences of local actions or future consequences of present actions. These often result in spatial biases of economic policies, sectoral priorities and regulations of economic activities, and the concen-

141 –

tration and over-building of the large cities in reaction to current pressures and demands.[55]

(v) Expansion of large cities: the rapid growth of the largest cities, during periods of concentration, results in a systematic overload on their infrastructure, and too great a demand on their supply of productive employment (that pays a living wage). Such pressures and expansion in demand result in expansion in the city's influence and functions into neighbouring urban and rural settlements, expansion of urban land uses into its often uncontrolled periphery, and expansion in informal sector activities, whether planned or not.

In effect, such autonomous processes signal a process of metropolitanization and spatial and functional differentiation and deconcentration within core regions, even when their national systems are still undergoing a process of concentration (Sao Paulo, Mexico City, Cairo, Seoul).[56] The guidance and control of such a process requires an expansion in the boundaries of planning over a much larger (regional) area, a high degree of administrative coordination and control of urban land development.

The Challenges of 'Counter-urbanization'

The challenges of the process of urban deconcentration can perhaps be discerned from the problems brought about by the recent 'counter-urbanization' processes in a number of MDCs. In doing so, however, one has to keep in perspective the uniqueness of certain elements of such experiences. The implications of the differences in spatial contexts, development approaches, cultural and historical roots on planning orientation can have major impacts on the resulting form and rate of deconcentration and spatial expansion of the urban system.[57] Furthermore, assumptions of unlimited growth, abundant resources, unchecked exploitative practices (at the international and national levels) and faith in unregulated market forces are no longer valid. Differences notwithstanding, deconcentration processes present the common challenges of promoting efficient patterns of urban and regional growth while at the same time maintaining a balanced distribution of welfare in face of structural and spatial shifts within the economy.

– 142

The policy challenge. The challenge to such a national policy role lies in its ability to:

(i) Monitor and define the complex linkages, structural changes and interdependencies within the emerging urban patterns and their implications for urban settlements;

(ii) Help smooth the process of technological and physical readjustment to emerging specialization and shifts in the traditional economic base of large cities;

(iii) Provide flexible mechanisms for adjusting and equalizing the levels of welfare in face of increasing spatial mobility and population redistribution patterns.

Policy issues. The major policy issues are as follows:

(i) Structural shifts in the economy: as economies mature, they undergo structural shifts that tend to undermine the traditional economic base of large cities, particularly manufacturing and trade activities. Employment in manufacturing begins to decline relatively in advanced, progressively service-oriented economies, e.g. the United Kingdom, the United States, the Federal Republic of Germany, France (Table 3.10). Such employment shifts are likely to be reinforced by further decreases in the rate of population growth and in agricultural employment, and by international shifts in manufacturing activities.[58] Furthermore, changes in the organization of markets and in methods of production will tend to favour locations outside large cities. The implications of such shifts for changes in the structure of employment and fiscal base of large cities, during the process of readjustment, pose major national and regional challenges.

(ii) Spatial shifts in welfare requirements: increased interurban mobility and deconcentration coupled with demographic changes in the national population (e.g. slow growth and changes in the age structure and in international migration) may have important implications for changes in demographic and social characteristics and for the spatial redistribution of welfare requirements among regions and urban centres. These imbalances have been found to increase the burdens of cities in the United States, France, the Federal Republic of Germany, and for Rio de Janeiro (as a result of government shift to Brasilia).[59] Their implications will vary significantly among countries and are, in large

Table 3.10. Structural Changes in National Economies of Selected OECD Countries, 1965-75

	1965 Number of Jobs (Millions)	1965 Percentage of Total in Nation	1970 Number of Jobs (Millions)	1970 Percentage of Total in Nation	1975 Number of Jobs (Millions)	1975 Percentage of Total in Nation
France						
Agriculture[1]	3.511	18.0	2.907	14.3	2.355	11.3
Industry[2]	7.823	40.0	8.065	39.5	8.022	38.5
Other[3]	8.210	42.0	9.420	46.2	10.467	50.2
Federal Republic of Germany						
Agriculture	2.876	10.9	2.262	8.5	1.823	7.4
Industry	12.792	48.4	12.679	48.5	11.408	46.0
Other	10.750	40.7	11.228	42.9	11.567	46.6
Italy						
Agriculture	4.898	26.0	3.613	19.5	2.964	15.8
Industry	1.659	40.7	8.117	43.8	8.305	44.1
Other	6.259	33.3	6.784	36.6	7.549	40.1
Japan						
Agriculture	11.130	23.5	8.860	17.4	6.610	12.7
Industry	15.330	32.4	18.190	35.7	18.730	35.9
Other	20.840	44.1	32.890	46.9	26.890	51.5
United Kingdom						
Agriculture	.952	3.8	.784	3.2	.668	2.7
Industry	11.536	46.6	10.913	44.8	10.018	40.7
Other	12.290	49.6	12.676	52.0	13.908	56.6
United States						
Agriculture	4.361	6.1	3.462	4.4	3.381	4.0
Industry	23.722	33.4	25.433	32.3	24.571	29.0
Other	43.005	60.5	49.732	63.3	56.831	67.0

[1]Agriculture includes agriculture, hunting, forestry and fishing.
[2]Industry includes mining and quarrying, manufacturing, electricity, gas and water and construction.
[3]Other includes wholesale and retail trade, restaurants and hotels, transport, storage and communication, financing, insurance, real estate and business services, community, social and personal services.

SOURCE: Organization for Economic Co-operation and Development, Economic Statistics and National Accounts Division, 'Labour Force Statistics', 1965-76, Paris 1978. From George A. Rigeluth, 'The Urban Implications of Changes in National Economic Structure in OECD Countries', Report to the Office of Policy Development and Research, US Department of Housing and Urban Development, Washington, DC, October 1979.

part, a function of prior national development policies and extent of urban concentration.

(iii) Incidence of physical and technological obsolescence: During periods of concentration and rapid growth, large metropolitan areas tend to become overbuilt in terms of capital plant and industrial infrastructure, and develop rigid patterns in terms of production technologies, work patterns, and property and political interests. These patterns may inhibit their responsiveness and ability to adapt to new economic realities, relatively reduce their competitiveness, and severely limit their capacity for renewal of their capital plant and employment base.[60]

(iv) Countering environmental and fiscal stress: while shifts in the national economy may produce new jobs equivalent to those replaced, it is clear that their geographic loci do not necessarily coincide, nor do the skills and work patterns of individuals concerned. Thus the growth in service and white-collar functions may not be able to compensate for losses in manufacturing and trade (Table 3.11). Such growth may also limit effective increases in cities' local revenue commensurate with increased levels of activity because of the changed nature of that activity. In their readjustment to new interdependencies within urban regions, large cities continue to carry a larger share of the burdens of congestion, environmental stresses and demands for services, while their revenues and political power tend to have a relative

Table 3.11. Estimated Employment Replacement Requirements for Constant Tax Revenues from Taxation of Non-Residential Property Business Income, Personal Income and Retail Sales*

Replaced Industry	Replacing Industry			
	Manufacturing	Wholesale and Retail Trade	Services	Government
Manufacturing	1.00	0.71	1.11	1.61
Wholesale and Retail Trade	1.42	1.00	1.57	2.28
Services	0.92	0.64	1.00	1.46
Government	0.62	0.44	0.69	1.00

*Calculated from business income, property and sales tax figures for 1969 and personal income tax figures for 1970.

SOURCE: Ray W. Bahl, Alan K. Campbell and David Greytak, *Taxes, Expenditure and the Economic Base: Case Study of New York*, (New York, Praeger, 1974), p. 151.

SALAH EL-SHAKHS

decline. They become increasingly dependent on provincal and national governments on these governments' policies on burden-sharing and reducing inequities in the transition process.

The Logic of Government Intervention

Maintaining and promoting national integration is a primary function of national governments. The impact of such a process, however, on development disparities (inter-regional, inter-urban, and inter-personal) depends to a large extent on the level of initial disparities in resources, levels of development, and effective shares in political power. In the absence of strong redistributive measures, therefore, greater integration could lead to either convergence or divergence within the national system, depending on its initial conditions. Thus national governments in both market and planned economies cannot be neutral in such a process.

Furthermore, greater integration and consequent information flows and exchange necessarily lead to stronger perceptions and awareness of such disparities and imbalances, thus increasing expectations and heightening conflicts.[61] These increasingly become an issue of national public policy and, under certain conditions, become a threat to national territorial integrity.[62]

The argument, therefore, is not whether national governments should intervene in the spatial development process, by actively promoting national integration (economic, spatial, and socio-political), but what type of role should they play in the process, when, and how? Traditional market forces do not operate, at least in the short run and particularly in LDCs, to create the equilibrating and optimizing mechanisms attributed to them by neo-classical economics, through the free flows of commodities and or factors of production.

Thus even if long-term economic and spatial convergence are an ultimate eventuality, there are compelling demographic, social and political reasons to guide it and speed it up through public policy. Such reasons include the imbalances between the rates of national population and economic growth, inefficient distribution of population in relation to resources and technological capacities, glaring spatial and social inequities in income and development levels, and the incapacity of local institutions and

– 146

resources to cope with the changing demands and complexities of urbanization and counter-urbanization processes.

If properly timed and designed, government intervention should enhance rather than retard balancing and equilibrating mechanisms in the development process. It should reduce the time-lag in inter-regional and inter-urban equilibrium mechanisms by moderating the differences in access to urbanization and scale economies. It should widen rather than restrict the freedom of choice of potential migrants by increasing viable alternative options, and their knowledge of them, including that of not migrating. Finally it should strengthen rather than weaken the local governments' ability to respond to local challenges and to manage and control their local resources effectively.

National and Regional Strategy Responses: an Assessment of Experience

Many governments have recognized that it would be both economically wasteful and politically and socially unacceptable, or intolerable, to wait patiently for an automatic polarization reversal process which would eventually significantly reduce regional disparities and the pressures on very large cities. Even if such acceptance of dependent integration and increased economic polarization, as an implicit or explicit development strategy, were to result in significant increases in GNP, experience of LDCs has shown that GNP growth often fails to improve the conditions of the poorest people in both rural and urban areas.[63] This 'growth without development' approach would also have adverse implications for the long-range economic efficiency of the system and the short-range functional and orderly development of the large cities.[64]

A recent survey indicated that 83 per cent of the LDCs (92 per cent in Latin America and 94 per cent in Africa) perceive the spatial distribution of their population as unacceptable.[65] Dissatisfaction with primate city patterns and recognition of the need to rationalize population–resource relationships focused attention on issues of regional development and the structure of the urban system, and the resulting spatial and hierarchical imbal-

147 –

Table 3.12. National and Regional Strategies and Policy Instruments Influencing the Future of Large Cities

(a) Indirect

Areas of Policy Impact	Major Issues	Policies, Programmes and Strategies	Policy Instruments		
			Economic	Political Social	Administrative/Institutional
Integration within the international economic system	Dependency relationships, extent of market, economic duality and appropriateness of technology and aid transfers.	Relative self-reliance and isolation. Open integration and specialization within international markets. Regional co-operation, common markets, joint projects and border area development.	Import substitution. Trade restrictions, tariffs, quotas and regulations. Foreign investment incentives, disincentives and controls. International transportation and communication links and interaction.	Migration control. International aid and co-operation and foreign policy. International scientific, cultural and technological exchange.	Monetary regulations. International assistance regulations. Lending, borrowing and debt regulations. Technical assistance, education, and professional and managerial exchange.
National integration and population and economic development.	International migration, labour and capital flows. Impact on nodes of international interaction, concentration in capital cities, dualism in city structure. International environmental protection and resource development, conservation and redistribution. Human resources development, quality of life, human rights and fertility control. Economic and political integration.	Family planning and human resources development programmes. Industrialization programmes and industrial decentralization. Administrative decentralization and distribution of decision-making powers. Agriculture and rural development programmes and land colonization.	Licensing and regulation of economic activities. Tax, wage and price laws and regulations. Loan, credit and banking regulations. Tax incentives, disincentives, grants and subsidies.	Land reform. Social and welfare services. Emancipation of women. Inheritance and family laws and civil regulations, marriage age, child support. Community organization and political development.	Land tenure and property regulations. Organization of planning (central, regional and local). Data collection, monitoring and dissemination. Deconcentration of national government offices and employment.

Areas of Policy Impact	Major Issues	Policies, Programmes and Strategies	Policy Instruments		
			Economic	Political/Social	Administrative/Institutional
Population distribution and regional development.	Regional disparities and balanced regional development. Population distribution, resource development and national economic efficiency. Rate and level of urbanization and its impact on economic development.	Income redistribution policies and programmes. Regional development programmes and special area projects (depressed areas, resource regions, frontier regions). Population movement and migration control. Concentrated decentralization of urban population (growth centres, development poles, new towns, new capital cities, regional centres and intermediate cities). Dispersal of urban services and activities (agropolitan development, central places). Closed city programmes.	Transportation, utilities and communication infrastructure. Manpower training, allocation and unemployment regulations. Informal sector regulations and organization. Direct investment and joint ventures. Labour-intensive technologies. Regional specialization.	Local and regional autonomy, local government and administrative organization and control. Local and regional identity and cultural development. Human resources development and training programmes. Regional information systems and mass media.	Technical assistance and extension services. Regional and local land-use planning, zoning and urban land controls. Population movement controls and restrictions. Regulations of access to housing, employment and social services. Adjustment of political and municipal boundaries.
The national urban hierarchy.	Urban concentration and primacy and their impact on the efficiency of the urban system. Expansion of the urban system, deconcentration, dispersal and their environmental and ecological impacts.		Regional wage differential. Industrial estates.	Revenue-sharing. Regionalization of the budget. Local tax and revenue control.	Designation of priority zones and development areas. Regulation of building standards and construction industry. Land banking and regulation of development rights.

Table 3.12. (Continued)

(b) Direct

			Policy Instruments		
Areas of Policy Impacts	Major Issues	Policies, Programmes and Strategies	Economic	Political/Social	Administrative/Institutional
Core region growth or decline.	Excessive concentration of population and economic activities.	No-growth and closed-city programmes.	Tax incentives and disincentives.	Neighbourhood organization and community participation.	Migration restrictions.
Core region settlement subsystem.	Extreme pressures on core regions' service systems and employment capacity.	Urban renewal and redevelopment.	Transportation policy and planning.	Local planning and control.	Area-wide planning, co-ordination and control.
Large city organization and efficiency.	Decline in quality of life and area disparities.	Regional deconcentration programmes (new towns, satellite cities, parallel cities, regional sub-centres).	Relocation of public functions.	Self-help programmes.	Administrative re-organization, annexation and adjustment of political boundaries.
	Expansion in urbanized area beyond city boundaries, control, co-ordination and planning.	Land-use planning and control.	Development ceilings on industrial and other economic activities.	Income support and social welfare programmes.	Employment and housing allocations and restrictions.
	Physical and technological obsolescence.	Community upgrading and redevelopment programmes.	Grants, loans, credits and subsidies.	Community identification.	Urban land controls, regulation and acquisition of land and of development rights.
	Gap between cost of land and services and ability to pay.	Urban revitalization, rehabilitation and conversion.	Economic specialization.	Land tenure systems.	Development priority zoning, targeting and designation.
	Decline in economic base, employment and revenue.	Regulation and organization of informal sector activities.	Industrial estates.	Regional co-operation, regional government and regionalized budget.	Rent controls, subsidies and regulation.
	Overcrowding, congestion and density; deterioration of services, utilities and amenities.	New towns in-town.	Direct investment and demonstration projects.	Relocation and resettlement programmes.	Building regulations and standards.
		Secondary business centres.	Employment generation.	Homesteading.	Land assembly and land banking.
		Concentrated development zones.		Neighbourhood associations and co-operatives.	Regulation and pricing of services and utilities.
		Green belts.			Spot renewal and demolition programmes.
					Regulation of construction industry.

ances. As a result many governments have attempted to influence inter-regional development patterns through indirect national policies or direct spatial development strategies, and nearly half of the LDCs formulated policies to modify the distribution of their urban population.[66]

The Nature of Responses

Levels and approaches of policies and instruments. National and regional policy responses to the challenges of urban concentration and deconcentration, and the attendant pressures and imbalances within urban systems, can generally be classified, in terms of their focus and impact, into three categories (Table 3.12):

(i) manipulation of the economic basis of development through transfer and distributional allocations and diffusion processes;

(ii) social and political development and integration processes at national, regional and local levels through political and governmental organization, distribution of decision-making power, initiative and participation and control of development;

(iii) institutional and administrative regulation of development and factor movements through legal and administrative controls, planning and budgeting.

Evaluation limitations. Evaluating the impact of such policies and strategies is an inherently difficult task for a number of reasons.

(i) Because spatial development patterns and objectives are constantly changing, it is difficult in most cases to distinguish between autonomous and policy-induced changes.[67] For instance, changes in such an important factor as regional income inequalities have been attributed to economic growth (see above), the political system (United States), or to intergovernmental fiscal system (Japan), rather than to any specific development policy or strategy.[68]

(ii) The economic impacts of development strategies are easier to measure than qualitative non-economic impacts. The former figures more prominently in most evaluative studies. Not only are the social, psychological, political and environmental impacts of development strategies as important as economic ones, if not more so, but it is also virtually impossible to base development strategies purely on economic engineering.[69]

(iii) The impacts of development strategies may be significantly delayed because of the lags in response in the development process. Thus they could not be evaluated merely on the basis of their short-term results, which may, in some instances, be contrary to their long-range impacts.

Evaluation of Basic Strategy Approaches

Decentralization through economic integration and diffusion approaches. Evaluations of experiences with regional development policies, whose basic thrust was to diffuse development outwards into peripheral areas through greater economic and spatial integration with core regions, indicate that they generally benefited the core more than the periphery.[70] Such strategies include growth centre outposts, decentralization of modern capital-intensive industry, improvements in inter-regional accessibility, and extension of core region service and organizational networks and standards. 'Consequently, peripheral areas, in addition to their increasing dependence on external production factors and external demand, also became increasingly dependent on external private and public decision-making.'[71]

Such regional development approaches thus tended to displace traditional and informal sector activities, benefit a limited group of the population, increase dependence and concentration focused on the core region, and undermine the capacity for local integrated internal development.

Socio-political development approaches. Experience indicates that economic decentralization and diffusion strategies would tend to succeed where inequalities are low, local governments are strong, and locational and resource endowments are high. The effects of inter-governmental fiscal relations (Japan, the Republic of Korea), regionalization of the budget (France, Sweden) and revenue sharing with a measure of local autonomy (Nigeria, the United States) indicate the importance of fiscal and administrative decentralization.

As a redistribution and equalization strategy, administrative decentralization has three distinct dimensions (or functions), economic, institutional and political. In an economic sense, it is a redistribution of public and government employment which, in most LDCs and centrally planned economies, accounts for a substantial proportion of total formal sector employment, personal income and purchasing power. Institutionally, it provides an important component of the social infrastructure and local organizational capacity, and it nurtures the creation of the demand for, and supply of, local services and amenities. Politically, its effect could range from the simple creation of a local bureaucratic constituency (an interest group within the national bureaucracy), to broadening the base of decision-making, participation and initiative (redistribution and devolution of power).

Concentration of fiscal and decision-making power strengthens that concentration process in the core region. Effective administrative decentralization, however, depends on the nature of the political system and the extent of broad-based social development and sharing in economic power. In many countries, e.g. in Latin America, progress in administrative decentralization is very slow and may be out of step with local realities. It requires a strong national commitment, co-ordination among national agencies and local governments, training and technical assistance, and a multi-level system of planning.[72]

Institutional controls and planning approaches. Experience with planning and implementing regional and urban development has been mixed. They are hard to enforce, particularly in LDCs, partly because enforcement mechanisms are weak, open to manipulation or non-existent, and partly because they often go against established trends. In the absence of tight control of different aspects of society (centrally planned economies) or existence of alternative outlets in the form of greater options of choice (MDCs), direct controls are likely to be ineffective. For example, Egypt periodically had to exempt all building violations from severe penalties in the face of an extreme housing shortage in the Cairo area.

Closed city programmes that seek to restrict migration to large cities (Soviet Union, Poland, China, Indonesia, Italy), to reduce or restrict additional investment (France, Egypt), to limit the growth of the informal sector (through harassment), to deport

153 –

illegal residents (the United Republic of Tanzania, the United States) or to deny them services (Philippines) have been only partly successful at best.[73] Efforts to remove squatters and non-licensed activities or to control the use of urban and agricultural land often meet with corruption and/or political pressure.

Planning efforts have frequently been preoccupied with the symptoms rather than the causes of urbanization problems, and tended to emphasize negative controls rather than positive adaptive approaches. This makes their implementation unlikely to be effective, even if the necessary administrative co-ordination, persistence and resources are available.

Limitations and Achievements of Urbanization Strategies

Strategies whose purpose is the creation of a more balanced distribution of urban growth have generally aimed at either 'concentrated-decentralization' from the top down, or broader-based dispersed urbanization from the bottom up. Both types have been primarily linked to issues of rural and regional development imbalances and primacy in LDCs. Urban revitalization strategies, on the other hand, are identified with the process of deconcentration and the decline of central cities in MDCs. The following brief review highlights some of the limitations and achievements of such strategies.

Growth centre strategies. These are intended to establish, at strategically selected locations, sufficiently large agglomeration economies focused on fast growing 'propulsive' firms linked to the regional economy. As these activities grow, they are supposed to stimulate the growth and development of the region through increasing demand for local products, providing local access to capital and technology, raising the local levels of employment and income, and diffusing growth impulses into their hinterlands. Ideally, then, these multiplier effects should largely be contained within the region and thus continuously upgrade its capacity to develop.

In practice, however, this did not seem to occur, partly because the 'propulsive' activities frequently were, by necessity or choice, branches of national or multi-national firms operating

Table 3.13. Demographic (1960) Correlates of Urban Change Rates, 1950–70
(Correlation coefficients over .15)*

National Characteristics in 1960	RATE OF CHANGE (1950–70) POPULATION						PRIMACY	
	Total	Largest City	Less than 100,000	100,000 to 499,999	500,000 to 1,000,000	Over 1,000,000	Largest City as Percentage of Total Urban	Largest City of Three Next-Largest
Total Population	−.27	−.36				.27	−.39	−.47
Urban Population	−.46	−.56					−.41	−.49
Population in Cities:								
Under 100,000	−.38	−.52		−.20			−.48	−.48
100,000–499,999	−.48	−.55		−.22			−.47	−.42
500,000–1,000,000	−.41	−.53		−.26			−.44	−.47
Over 1,000,000	−.45	−.52		−.29			−.39	−.43
Percentage of Total Population in Cities:								
Under 100,000	−.17		−.19	.19		−.41		
100,000–499,999	−.50	−.27	−.17		−.25	−.55		
500,000–1,000,000	−.38	−.36	−.41			−.40		
Over 1,000,000			−.34		.18	−.34		
Population of Largest City	−.51	−.56	−.25	−.24		−.31	−.25	−.34
Largest City as Percentage of:								
(1) Total Urban Population	.41	.25		.20			.18	.27
(2) Three Next-Largest	.17		−.27	.22		−.23		

*These are Pearson coefficients, based on data for the 33 nations predicted to have at least one city having over 5 million population by the year 2000. All coefficients are based on at least 67 percent of this maximum number of nations, and most pertain to all 33 identified in Table 5.3.

SALAH EL-SHAKHS

within pre-existing linkage networks and controlled from outside
the region, and partly because of low levels of physical and economic integration within these regions. Thus they frequently
turned into enclaves which, even if successful within their own
urban settlement boundaries, failed to induce the intended development in their hinterlands at least in the short run (Malaysia,
Mexico, Brazil, Ireland, Japan).[75] In some instances they have
had detrimental effects on their hinterland, by siphoning off their
capital and more skilled labour (Kenya), and by displacing traditional informal sector activities.[76]

Relative success of growth centres in attracting population, or
diverting migration, seems to have been higher in cases of small
countries (Israel, the Netherlands), higher in proximity to large
cities within core regions (Brazil), and higher in MDCs with relatively low rural-urban inequalities (Federal Republic of Germany), or in centrally planned economies (Soviet Union). In general, their performance is influenced by the extent of political and
administrative decentralization, the extent of supporting developments in social and physical infrastructure, the extent of
complementary integrated development in their hinterlands, and
the degree of dependency and concentration within their national
systems.

Growth centres may be relatively expensive and ineffectual (in
terms of regional impacts) in the short run; however, given time
and commitment, well-selected centres (or development towns)
could eventually help fill the gaps in the urban hierarchy and
provide a balanced structure for inter-regional deconcentration.
Further, concentrated development on a moderate scale (based
on the growth centre notion) may provide useful tools for the
synchronization and co-ordination of visible high-impact projects
in potentially growing secondary centres, e.g. zones of urban
priority (France), designated development areas (Republic of
Korea), industrial estates, etc.

Intermediate cities and regional centres: counter-primacy.
Maximizing the benefits and minimizing the costs of growth
centre strategies, in LDCs undergoing a concentration process,
would largely depend on the choice of their locations and the
type and mix of activities. Where the goal is to counter the primacy of the largest cities, in a step-wise process of urban decon-
– *156*

centration, already established cities with adequate levels of service and administrative infrastructure seem to provide a better chance of success for such strategies.

The size, location and function of cities plays an important role in the identification of likely candidates. Spontaneously growing cities, where additional stimulus and administrative organization and co-ordination would have a major impact, provide appropriate targets 'since policies can swim with the stream much more effectively than against it.'[77] Such cities usually fall in the second tier in terms of function and size group, and are strategically located within the transportation and communication network, either nationally or within relatively independent large regional subsystems. They include regional and administrative centres and secondary centres of specialized economic activities (e.g. ports, mineral or hydroelectric resources, religious or cultural centres, resort areas, etc.). Their sizes vary with city size distributional characteristics (over 100,000 in Brazil, Mexico, Egypt, India, the Philippines and the Republic of Korea; less than that in Nigeria and Indonesia, and over half a million in Japan).

The growth of intermediate-sized cities has been associated not only with industrial decentralization (industrial estates, tax incentives and preferential treatment), but perhaps more importantly with the growth in tertiary activities (services, wholesale trade and government employment, as was the case in Nigeria, Brazil and Japan), and a greater local control over resources and the budget. This is particularly the case when intermediate cities are not located close to the largest city; that is, where they serve as satellite extensions within an expanding core region.

New towns and satellite cities. Few countries have developed comprehensive and sustained new town programmes at the national level (notably the United Kingdom, the Soviet Union and Israel). Many more have had isolated instances of new town developments or new capital cities, for a large variety of reasons and objectives. Experience indicates that there are three basic approaches to new town strategies:

(i) As development towns or growth centres in underdeveloped resource regions, declining regions, or sparsely populated frontier regions, with a primary focus on regional development.[78]

SALAH EL-SHAKHS

(ii) As counter-magnets for decentralization of development and deconcentration of population and activities, diverting migration away from core regions or deconcentrating large primate cities, with a primary forcus on balancing the urban hierarchy.[79]

(iii) As large-scale integrated communities to organize the internal spatial structure and expansion of metropolitan areas and form an integral part of the metropolitan labour and housing markets, with a primary focus on rationalizing the development and expansion of urban regions.[80]

New towns or cities that are not an integral part of expanding metropolitan areas or large cities face the same constraints and problems of growth centres. In addition, they require major capital investments, sustained governmental support and subsidies over long periods of time, and efficient methods of financing and management. This raises serious questions about the effectiveness of new towns, outside the zones of metropolitan influence, as an approach of expanding the urban systems of LDCs. In order to attract managerial and skilled populations, their design and construction standards are usually high and thus tend to exclude or neglect those with the lowest incomes. Their absorption capacity, even in large-scale programmes, is limited to a fraction of total urban population growth, which may not justify their high cost. Such resources may be more effectively used to diffuse urban services and infrastructure into small urban centres and integrated industrial-rural service central places.[81]

Within metropolitan areas and expanding core regions, however, new towns may present a sound approach for planned deconcentration. Polarization reversal in spatial systems is likely to be preceded by spatial reorganization trends in core regions themselves. This process involves the spatial differentiation and deconcentration of core regions' population and activities, over a larger area, as central cities expand their economic interactions into their hinterlands. Usually, this takes place during their periods of rapid growth and expansion accompanied by intensified transportation and communication developments. The beginning of the outward spatial expansion and dispersal of core regions signals the onset of the impact of diseconomies of concentration in the large central cities. Peripheral areas in the region, having been made more accessible, gain in comparative locational ad-

– 158

Table 3.14. Regional Inequality and National Performance Correlates of the Urban Hierarchy, since 1960

(Correlation coefficients, number of nations in parentheses)

Per cent of Total Population In Cities, By Size 1960 or 1970[5]	National Real Product Growth Rate[1]		Inequality Index		Change In Regional Inequality (Per cent)[4]
	1960–70	1970–77	Regional[2]	National[3]	
Per cent of Total Population In Cities, By Size 1960 or 1970[5]					
I. Under 100,000	–.13 (17)	.08 (17)	.06 (14)	.03 (26)	
II. 100,000–499,999	–.15 (17)	.17 (17)	–.37 (14)	–.09 (26)	
III. 500,000–1,000,000	–.13 (17)	.33 (17)	–.25 (14)	–.27 (26)	
IV. Over 1,000,000	.72 (17)	.25 (17)	–.23 (14)	–.15 (26)	
Growth Rate of Population in Cities, By Size 1960–70:					
I. Under 100,000	.04 (16)		.08 (12)	–.13 (25)	.45 (8)
II. 100,000–499,999	–.12 (16)		.47 (12)	.43 (25)	–.01 (8)
III. 500,000–1,000,000	.26 (11)		.29 (10)	.32 (18)	–.11 (8)
IV. Over 1,000,000	–.30 (12)		.67 (12)	.60 (24)	.18 (8)
Growth Rate of Percentage of Total Population in Cities, 1960–70:					
I. Under 100,000	.03 (16)		–.43 (12)	–.42 (25)	.16 (8)
II. 100,000–499,999	–.12 (16)		.09 (12)	.36 (25)	–.14 (8)
III. 500,000–1,000,000	.28 (11)		.18 (10)	–.39 (18)	–.12 (8)
IV. Over 1,000,000	–.25 (12)		.54 (12)	.46 (24)	.16 (8)

[1] This is the growth rate in the constant dollar value of the gross domestic product.

[2] The regional inequality index is the coefficient of variation. Regional per capita incomes are weighted according to the relative population size of each. The first four rows utilize available indices for the years generally since 1970. The last eight rows utilize comparable indices estimated for various years between 1950 and 1960, by Williamson. Note that this index declines as equality increases.

[3] The aggregate national income inequality index is the Gini coefficient estimated by Jain for various years, primarily since 1960. This index declines as equality increases.

[4] Regional inequality indices were available for two successive points in time (1950s and 1970s) for just eight nations. There may be minor differences in the regionalizations used at successive times; consequently the indices may not be exactly comparable.

[5] Cities may change from one size class to another over time. The first column uses this population data for 1960, while the remaining columns use 1970 population data.

SOURCE: Jeffrey G. Williamson, 'Regional Inequality and the Process of National Development: A Description of Patterns', *Economic Development and Social Change* 13, July 1965, 3–45, for the data base on regional inequality indices for the period 1950–60.

vantages for an increasing number of activities, led by large industries. As population disperses it creates more incentives and markets for other consumption and service-oriented activities to follow suit.

In this process of intra-regional reorganization, large-scale integrated new towns or expanded towns would have little problem in attracting population and economic activities, since they are economically and psychologically integral parts of the core regions. If well planned at a regional level, such settlements can reduce the cost of development and pressures on the large city in the short run, and minimize the long-range impacts of autonomous deconcentration.

Several countries have shifted their capitals away from large primate cities (Brazil, Cameroon, Libya, Turkey, Pakistan) and several more are contemplating or planning such a shift (including Nigeria and the United Republic of Tanzania). New capitals are special projects often motivated by political, symbolic and demonstration objectives.[82] Although their objectives may include hinterland development (Brasilia, Ankara, Dodoma) and counterprimacy (Abuja, Dodoma), the nature of such projects places them outside the realm of more general urban development strategies. From a strictly spatial development perspective they are too drastic, costly and risky an alternative, and do not necessarily lead to deconcentration trends either in the spatial system or in the primate city.[83]

Dispersed urbanization: the bottom-up strategy. There is little experience, and even less information, on large-scale strategies intended to spread urbanization right at its point of origin: in rural areas. Most rural development policies have focused on raising productivity and social development levels in rural areas, through central government initiatives, policies and institutions. Frequently, this involved the establishment of growth centres or the designation of central places. The impact of such strategies of diffusion, under conditions of rapid rural population growth during stages of concentration, have generally not helped develop a grass-roots dispersed urbanization; they have even increased the pace of migration to large urban centres.[84]

The United Republic of Tanzania's approach of initiating development at the *ujamaa* level and promoting concentrated urban development in eight designated intermediate towns represents a mixture of both decentralized and dispersed urban strategies. Its original (1967) intent was to promote a self-reliant development at both local and regional levels, and to promote decentralization of responsibility and of decision-making power. Problems of inter-regional economic variations, decline in output of some major cereal crops, and some peasant reluctance to form *ujamaas,* however, resulted in greater central government coercions by 1974, undermining the concept of self-reliance. Furthermore, linking rural and urban development within the *ujamaa* concept has not worked out thoroughly.[85]

Reconciling self-reliance and autonomy with the central government's role and assistance, and reconciling dispersed urbanization with an efficient urban hierarchy, constitute unresolved issues of such a strategy. They are issues that are specific to each political and spatial context. In the early experience of Israel's development towns, for example, it was found out that the unique direct interaction between the self-reliant kibbutzim and the large urban centres (resulting from small geographic size and relatively well-developed marketing and communications networks) left little room for the role and function of intermediate central places.[86] A multi-tiered hierarchy and regional closure may be irrelevant under such conditions.

Generally, however, grass-roots urbanization is being advocated in strategies that essentially aim at containing the forces of increased dependency and inter-regional mobility within the spatial system. Such strategies include integrated rural development, regional closure, self-reliance, local initiative and control, and strong distributive measures.[87]

Urban revitalization strategies. While the above strategies are all concerned with initiating and spreading development outside core regions, urban revitalization strategies focus on minimizing the adverse impact of deconcentration on large cities. At the regional and national levels, this calls for more administrative coordination, area-wide planning and government responsibility. The increased levels of interdependency and inter-urban mobility, within an expanded deconcentrated urban settlement system, tend to shift the locus of effective policies from the city or

161 –

metropolitan level to both higher and lower levels of government.

Experience with large-city revitalization strategies are relatively recent and remain, to a large extent, experimental. They range from regional and state planning and co-operative efforts, through subsidies and grants for economic and community redevelopment programmes, to direct redistribution of income and revenue to states and municipalities.

Urban revitalization programmes in the United States began in the 1950s, in reaction to suburbanization and the decline of central business districts in older cities, with urban renewal efforts intended to rejuvenate the physical and economic health of such centres. Urban renewal efforts were largely unsuccessful, partly because of the resulting massive dislocations and disturbances, partly because they attempted to reverse deconcentration shifts (which were at the same time being accelerated by other government programmes and policies), and partly because they lacked community inputs. Subsequent efforts emphasized community participation and integrated development through targeted model city areas, direct community development grants, revenue sharing and adaptive reuse programmes.[88] Their intended effect is to improve housing and infrastructure and, more generally, the quality of city life. Such programmes, however, are localized in nature, and do not adequately address inter-urban imbalances, specialization and changes in relative competitive advantages within the national and international economies.

In addition to local renewal, conversion and reuse adaptations, flexible regional and national co-ordination and guidance of economic development policies, with specific spatial impacts, are essential for an efficient and equitable process of readjustment. The increased mobility and integration within the national system make it increasingly necessary for central government to assume major responsibilities for basic social welfare and service functions across the system. Pre-planning for deconcentration at national and broad regional levels, either through co-operation (Stockholm region) or formal plans (the Paris region, Singapore) would help anticipate and ease the process of adjustment.[89] In essence, continuous planning efforts, or lack of them, and the responsiveness and flexibility of institutions and strategies, will largely determine future urban challenges and humankind's capacity to face them.

Facing the Challenge: Frameworks for Policy

It is clear that 'the scene of the urban future' will not be set in the great metropolitan centres of the developed world but rather, it will be set in the Third World.'[90] Facing its challenge will require some hard political and economic choices both on the part of the community of nations as a whole and on that of national governments. The focus of spatial development policy should no longer be maintaining equilibrium, or the *status quo,* but rather promoting balanced inter-dependence.

Urban population distribution is a function of many dynamic and complex relationships and conditions. This makes it difficult to prescribe an optimum or a balanced hierarchy at a given point in time. However, policies should focus on broad ranges of distributional characteristics, the rate and direction of relative changes within the spatial system. Since rural and urban population distribution imbalances can ultimately be assessed by their impact on relative development levels, and are in turn affected by them, it is developmental imbalances that should become the explicit objectives of public policy and planning efforts.

Continued economic growth is a necessary but not a sufficient condition for reducing spatial and social disparities. While a certain degree of disparity may be inevitable, if the gross national product is to grow rapidly at early stages of development, policies should aim at reducing and containing such disparities within tolerable limits. The need to trade-off efficiency for equity can be minimized by broadening the natural resource base for development planning, and strengthening the forces of horizontal spatial expansion and integration.[91] In terms of national policy, this suggests several points.

(i) More attention and priority should be given to efforts whose aim is to develop human resources, in a broader sense, and to improve the quality of life and meet basic human needs.

(ii) Direct efforts aimed at decreasing the rate of natural increase of population should be intensified through greater access to suitable family planning services, information, education and acceptable methods of fertility regulation.

(iii) Fertility reduction efforts, beyond family planning, should become an integral part of the planning for human settlements in rural areas and for the urban poor, and should aim at improving income and quality of life of the family and the status of women.[92]

(iv) Spatial development objectives should become an integral part of national economic and social development policies and plans.

(v) Efforts of national integration should enhance and broaden the base of local and regional decision-making power, administrative efficiency, and community participation and initiative.

(vi) Development planning efforts should be articulated in terms of functionally integrated, relatively autonomous (economically and administratively) spatial subsystems at both regional and local levels, including integrated rural subsystems.

(vii) Central governments should play an explicit balancing and facilitating role in the processes of spatial transition and regional adjustments through development and communication of basic information on population and economic activities, organization and education for planning, technical and fiscal support, and regionalization of planning and budgeting.

(viii) Demographic, social and pyschological variables and objectives of population development should become integral parts of the planning and implementation process.

THE NATIONAL URBAN SETTLEMENT SYSTEM

Spatial expansion and integration of the national economy require an expanded and efficient urban settlement system. The development of such a system during the early stages of growth, particularly in large countries, requires conscious efforts and policies aimed at strengthening the economic, institutional and psychological basis for local and regional development. Fostering local integration and identity, and creating a cultural milieu that enhances local pride and creative power, would help counter the polarization forces of national integration within the urban system.[93]

One of the most sensitive and delicate policy choices, particularly for large, densely populated and diverse countries, is the need to balance the regionalization of development with the promotion of national integration. Such balance is particularly crucial in market and mixed economies, where spatial development can be guided through promoting options for, and influencing, individual choices, in contrast to controlling it through limited choices and planned inevitabilities in centrally planned economies.

Direct controls and restrictions of population movement, despite their relative success in a few instances, may have long-range undesirable demographic and economic consequences both for the largest cities and for the rest of the spatial system. Furthermore, they are difficult to enforce in most cases, particularly with increased accessibility and efforts towards national integration in LDCs.

What is required in these cases, therefore, seems to be the initiation of a step-wise process of integration in which:

(i) efforts to improve intra-regional accessibility within and among peripheral regions and to help promote local regional integration and increase aggregate demand would take precedence over inter-regional and national spatial and economic integration efforts;

(ii) the enrichment of social and cultural amenities and basic services in small urban places and regional centres, primarily through the redistribution of government and public sector facilities and employment opportunities among regions and urban settlements, would take precedence over redistribution of modern industrial activities;

(iii) industrial development strategies would promote competitive specialization among sub-national and regional centres on the basis of their locational advantages or regional resource base, rather than cheap labour;

(iv) administrative decentralization would genuinely strengthen the redistribution of decision-making power and control over resources, budget allocations and development efforts to strengthen local identity, initiative and participation.

Approaches for integrated rural-urban development in LDCs. A number of spatial development approaches have recently advocated strategies aimed at moderating rural-urban and inter-regional disparities which result from national integration efforts in LDCs.

(i) Integrated rural development: approaches of integrated rural development focus on raising the productivity of the average farmer, creating greater access to economic opportunity for the rural poor, and generally emphasize human resource development and raising the farmer's income and demand for consumer goods.[94] Such programmes should be locally organized with the participation of the farmers and focus on land reform and access to credit and to local urban services.

The small farmer, rather than the rich and large landowner, should be the prime beneficiary of these integrated efforts. In most cases, this should help fulfil the twin objectives of localization of development (and of urbanization) and increase in agricultural production.

Comparisons of average yields per acre by farm size indicate that labour-intensive productivity of small farms is much higher in many countries, including Argentina, Brazil, Chile, Colombia, Ecuador, Guatemala, Egypt and Thailand.[95] In fact it is reported that output per acre of basic food grains in Egypt is higher than in the United States and most developed countries, despite the fact that the average land holding is smaller.[96]

(ii) Agropolitan development: the success of integrated rural development will both require and enhance rural-urban integration and the localization of urbanization. One approach to achieve such integration is Friedmann's 'agropolitan development).[97] It advocates the creation of integrated districts, with central place-type urban functions unified with village populations in proximate spatial networks, each of which has suficient economic resources and autonomy to initiate and control its own development.

The spatial form and size of such units could vary among countries, but the basic requirements of such an approach are unity, autonomy and relative independence from the intrusion of large, western-oriented, modern, urban-industrial development forces. This would help localize development effects and reduce unnecessary and rapid displacement of traditional industry and informal sector activities.

(iii) Selective regional self-reliance: Self-reliant development has been advocated, by Stör and Palme, particularly for large, isolated, dense, undeveloped rural regions as a step-wise process of integration.[98] In this process, internal mobilization and development, with 'only subsidary external help and no strings attached', would precede any close functional and spatial integration within the national system. Such a strategy would emphasize broad access to land, priority for basic needs' projects, and a high degree of autonomy in decision-making and planning.

External links, in terms of both assistance and posible export activities, would also focus on internal development needs (internal communications and basic needs, and specialized resources and labour-intensive, small-scale, locally initiated industries). The role and distribution of urban functions and urban centres would thus become more of an integral part of their region's development than subordinate outposts of large national urban centres. The basic difference is one of orientation, relative strengths of linkages, and degree of autonomy and regional consciousness.

Counter-primacy approaches. While integrated rural-urban development efforts are essential (particularly in Type I countries), additional efforts to narrow the inequities within the urban settlement system are necessary. This is particularly true in small countries and countries that already have high degrees of urban concentration at the national level (Type II countries). In these cases a step-wise deconcentration effort (first inter-regional and subsequently intra-regional) should be pursued simultaneously with local integrated development. They should focus on well-established and autonomously growing specialized and/or regional urban centres (see above).

The success of such efforts, however, requires development principles, and a development sequence, similar to those of local integrated approaches. These include emphasis on regional autonomy, physical and social infrastructure development, income redistribution, local participation and initiative, and general improvemets in the quality of life and business environment. Deconcentration of national government functions and employment along with decentralization of decision-making powers, would be supportive of such efforts.

Such improvements would enhance the chances for subse-

167 –

quent decentralization of some industries and economic activities. The types of appropriate economic activities will obviously vary among selected cities, based on their region's resource base, size of market, and general economic conditions, and over time, with the city's growth and economic development. Initially, however, the selection should generaly avoid those industries that would displace traditional and informal sector activities and employment, that are closely linked to the core region's industries, market and power structure, that are primarily oriented towards export, or that are capital-intensive. This should help minimize backwash effects and inefficiences of forced decentralization of modern national industries out of the core region. The latter can perhaps be more readily decentralized within the core region subsystem as a prelude to their own deconcentration and the horizontal expansion of urban regions.

Coping with deconcentration in the MDCs. The first stage of any national urban development policy in mature urban systems is the formulation of integrated long-term national economic goals and strategies, both domestic and and international, to cope with their emerging role and shifting comparative advantage within the world economy. Within this framework, international trade policies must be reconciled with the existing urban and regional economic base, needs and potentials.

The above elements are closely inter-related. Decisions on national economic specializations or tracks (aero-space or computers, for example) and trade policies strongly influence regional, metropolitan and urban development patterns and differentials. Explicit recognition must be made of these complex linkages and inter-relationships, and reconciliations attempted within the fabric of national economic strategies.

Concurrently, a national balanced urban and regional growth policy should be formulated, employing national government investments and incentives directly to operationalize specific objectives. Persistent inter-regional and urban-suburban inequities may have to be alleviated with permanent revenue- and burden-sharing on the national level. Long-term readjustments emanating from the forces restructuring urban and regional patterns must be reconciled with policies easing the transitions taking place.

Within a national economic goal matrix, then, specific policies would seek to intervene in the process of national resource allocation while concurrently attempting to modify regional and urban environments, and infrastructures, tailoring them to future specializations and economic and market requirements. The role of the national government and impact of national policies increases rather than decreases under such conditions.

The Core Region Settlement Subsystem

The factors influencing the future of the large city and its region will largely be determined by the development of the urban system as a whole. However, the severity of the impacts of concentration and deconcentration trends on the city and its region are, in large part, a function of their internal spatial organization, and their planning and efficient management as a unit.

In both growing and declining core regions, administrative and political boundaries have lost their meaning. In either case, a large and growing proportion of the metropolitan area's population lives outside the city boundary, yet they frequently use its services without contributing to its resources or being influenced by its management. The processes of concentration and dispersions, and their consequent pressures and conflicts, within the core region are not only inequitable and difficult to manage but could also be extremely wasteful without planning and coordination at the regional level.

Thus the first step in facing the future challenge is to establish meaningful and workable mechanisms for region-wide planning and administrative co-ordination and control of development. Such mechanisms and institutions should be flexible enough so that their authority and its boundary could be expanded to fit those of the phenomena.

While spatial polarization may be inevitable within the national urban system, this need not be the case within the core region. Appropriate long-range plans should anticipate and organize the spatial and economic differentiation of the core region's expansion. Unlike the conventional wisdom of attempting to limit forcibly core regions' growth and physical expansion, this would call for recognizing and directing such expansion in ways that suit their particular spatial context. Such plans should provide an alternative to the excessive physical expansion of the large central city itself, to dispersed patterns that are expensive to serve and wasteful of energy, and to uncontrolled expansion into valuable farm land, ecologically sensitive areas or natural features worthy of preservation for a better use.

Generally speaking, a more efficient spatial organization can be achieved through:

(i) containing the horizontal expansion of the central city both by the application of efficient methods of land development and conservation controls, on the one hand, and by increasing the supply of accessible urban land (with provisions for basic utilities and services, around pre-determined existing or new activity and development centres) within the framework of horizontal expansion of the urban region subsystem, on the other;

(ii) establishing appropriate long-range plans for the spatial reorganization and differentiation of functions as a guide for the inevitable development of future urban regions focusing on corridors of intense interactions between major urban centres (within the national urban system and between countries).

(iii) restructing the peripheral areas through the promotion of subcentres, concentrated development zones, and linear expansion schemes based on transportation, site and service schemes, and deconcentration of public investments;

(iv) recognition and stabilization of spontaneous peripheral settlements, creation of intra-regional development centres around existing nuclei, and strengthening the identity and local economic and administrative initiative and autonomy within an expanded planning and co-ordinative function;

(v) rationalizing the internal structure of central cities in a poly-nucleated pattern by identifying and strengthening established communities around viable business sub-centres in the form of integrated towns-in-town;

(vi) encouraging area-wide differentiation of functions and specialization of the main centre and secondary centres through incremental long-range conversion, renovation and adaptive reuse programmes.

The polycentric spatial organization approach is a flexible strategy adaptable to future uncertainties. It would both anticipate the probable long-range trends of intra-regional deconcentration, or help organize metropolitan regions along manageable and humane dimensions, were they destined to continue their unabated growth for long periods in the future. Furthermore, while such an organization would help moderate the pressures of concentration within the metropolitan region, it would not compromise its economic efficiency.

The Political and Planning Challenge

It is clear that spatial inequalities in welfare contribute to, and are influenced by, urban concentration and deconcentration trends. In effect, equalizing levels of welfare, and quality of life, among different regions and urban centres would not only contribute to moderating such processes but also help eliminate the major cause for many local urban problems. While a move towards such equalization may indeed result from long-range sustained economic growth, it appears that aggregate regional equality does not necessarily imply interpersonal equality, particularly for the very poor. Additionally, the short-term effect of economic growth tends to be an increase in inequalities, in the case of LDCs. In mature urban systems, deconcentration and increased mobility also lead to inter-urban inequalities, at least in the short run, as a result of differential mobility rates and shifts in economic base.

In both cases, therefore, national and state governments should assume, either directly or through strong redistributive measures, responsibility for short-term satisfaction of a basic minimum level of social welfare across regional and municipal boundaries, and long-range equalization of such levels. Similar goals should guide the specific objectives of international aid, and technical assistance programmes of international agencies, in dealing with priorities and channeling of development efforts both among and within nations.

There will continue to be an urgent need for a true partnership in development efforts and planning, at all levels, based on principles of equity and participation. The impact of the system of international exchange on the capacities and prospects of internal national development, particularly in the LDCs, has increasingly become a subject of concern. In so far as it perpetuates international dependencies it will reinforce dependency relationships and inequalities within national economic and spatial systems. The resulting environmental, economic, social and political problems and conflicts, however, increasingly recognize no boundaries.

Large cities, particularly capital cities, are elements in an international network of 'world cities'. They reap the benefits and suffer the consequences of such exchange.[99] Their future is inextricably linked to developments both inside and outside their national systems. Therefore their well-being, in both the short and long term, depends on multi-level co-operation and planning (international, national, regional and local) based on:

(i) efforts to reduce social and spatial inequalities;

(ii) integrated development focusing on population and social development;

(iii) development of local and regional consciousness, initiative and participation;

(iv) redistribution of effective decision-making power;

(v) establishing efficient information gathering, monitoring and disseminating systems;

(vi) continuous exchange of experience and technical know-how among countries and large cities;

(vii) establishing land-use planning and control at a regional level with the necessary administrative reorganization or coordination mechanisms;

(viii) rationalizing land tenure systems and urban land policies, regulations, and controls in ways that would encourage self-help initiatives and investments;

(ix) rationalizing and assisting the informal sector through access to credit and capital, technical aid and training, market protection and government purchasing policies.

It is all too easy to recommend that governments should act on all these fronts and at all levels all the time. However, the realities of system linkages and interactions and of resource constraints, even in advanced nations, will always force upon us the central issues of planning: the necessity for trade-offs, the need to systematize priorities in a dynamic and responsible way over time, and the balance between satisfying immediate needs and maximizing long-term achievements.

Notes

1. A. H. Walsh, *The Urban Challenge to Government: An International Comparison of Thirteen Cities* (New York: Praeger Publishers, 1969).
2. United Nations, Economic and Social Council, 'Policies on Human Settlements in Latin America', Latin American Conference on Human Settlements, Mexico City, November 1979, p. 25.
3. W. A. Robson and D. Regan, *Great Cities of the World: Their Government, Politics and Planning* (London: George Allen and Unwin Ltd, 1972).
4. Walsh, *The Urban Challenge, op. cit.,* pp. 217–18.
5. Ibid.
6. B. J. Berry, *Urbanization and Counter-Urbanization* (Beverly Hills: Sage Publications, 1976), pp. 7–14.
7. W. Stöhr, 'Evaluation of Some Arguments Against Government Intervention to Influence Territorial Population Distribution', paper presented at United Nations/United Nations Fund for Population Activities Workshop on Population Distribution Policies, Bangkok, September 1979
8. G. Beier, *et al.,* 'The Task Ahead for Cities of the Developing Countries', Washington, World Bank Staff Working Paper No. 209, July 1975, pp. 4–5; B. Renaud, 'National Urbanization Policies in Developing Nations', Washington, World Bank Staff Working Paper No. 347, July 1979, pp. 35–50; UNFPA, 'Summary' and 'Introduction' to papers on Population Distribution Policies in Developing Countries, New York, 1979, pp. 6–8.
9. W. Stöhr, *Regional Development Experiences and Prospects in Latin America,* UNRISD Series on Regional Planning (The Hague: Mouton, 1975, 1977), p. 78; Renaud, 'National Urbanization Policies', *op. cit.,* p. 112.
10. United Nations, Department of Economic and Social Affairs, *Indicators of the Quality of Urban Development* (New York: United Nations, 1977), p. 9.
11. S. El-Shakhs, 'The Urban Crisis in International Perspective: The Challenge and the Response', *American Behavioral Scientist* 15 (March/April 1972): 581–90; Stöhr, *op. cit.,* 'Evaluation of Some Arguments Against Government Intervention'.
12. J. Abu-Lughod, 'The Urban Future: A Necessary Nightmare', paper presented at Rutgers University, April 1977, p. 8; R. Cuca, 'Family Planning Programs: An Evaluation of Experience', Washington, World Bank Staff Working Paper No. 345, July 1979, p. 39 and Table 5 (p. 40).
13. Renaud, 'National Urbanization', *op. cit.,* pp. 14–22; H. Richardson, 'City Size and National Spatial Strategies in Developing Countries', Washington, World Bank Staff Working Paper No. 252, April 1977.
14. L. A. P. Gosling and L. Y. C. Lim, eds, *Population Redistribution: Patterns, Policies and Prospects,* Policy Development Studies No. 2 (New York: UNFPA, 1979), p. 19.

15. These differences are usually attributed to demographic imbalances and assymetrical development. See, among others: Richardson, 'City Size', *op. cit.*, pp. 5, 18–23; Berry, *Urbanization and Counter-Urbanization;* J. Abu-Lughod and R. Hay, Jr, eds, *Third World Urbanization* (Chicago: Maaroufa Press, 1977).

16. D. R. Vining, Jr and T. Kontuly, 'Population Dispersal from Major Metropolitan Regions: An International Comparison', *International Regional Science Review* 3 (1978): 49–73.

17. Renaud, 'National Urbanization', *op. cit.*, pp. 128–30; S. El-Shakhs, 'Development, Primacy and Systems of Cities', *Journal of Developing Areas* 7 (October 1972): 30.

18. J. Williamson, 'Regional Inequality and the Process of National Development – A Description of Patterns', *Economic Development and Cultural Change* 13 (July 1965); K. Mera, 'Population Concentration and Regional Income Disparities: A Comparative Analysis of Japan and Korea', in *Human Settlement Systems*, ed N. Hansen (Cambridge, Massachusetts: Ballinger, 1978); W. Alonso, 'Income Inequalities Among Regions in the Long Run – A Theoretical Note', International Institute of Applied Systems Analysis, 1978.

19. A. L. Mabogunje, *Urbanization in Nigeria* (New York: Africana Press, 1978); L. Green and V. Milone, 'Urbanization in Nigeria: A Planning Commentary', International Urbanization Survey, the Ford Foundation, 1974; I. I. U. Eye, 'Population of Nigeria, 1952–1963', *Nigerian Journal of Economic and Social Studies* 8 (July 1966); J. C. Caldwell and A. A. Igun, 'The Population Outlook in Nigeria', seminar on Population Problems and Policy in Nigeria, Demographic Research and Training Unit, Ife University, March 1971; A. T. Salau, 'Urbanization, Planning and Public Policies in Nigeria', in *Development of Urban Systems in Africa*, ed R. Obudho and S. El-Shakhs (New York: Praeger, 1979), pp. 196–209.

20. A. T. Salau, 'Evaluating the Impact of Administrative Centralization on Regional Development in Nigeria as an Alternative Growth Center Strategy', (PhD dissertation, Rutgers University, 1979); A. Mabogunje, 'The Urban Situation in Nigeria', in *Patterns of Urbanization: Comparative Country Studies*, ed S. Goldstein and D. Sly, vol. 2 (Belgium: Ordina Editions, 1976).

21. C. Rosser, 'Urbanization in India', International Urbanization Survey, The Ford Foundation, 1971; A. Bose, 'Urbanization in India: A Demographic Perspective', in *Patterns of Urbanization*, ed Goldstein and Sly, Vol. 1, pp. 289–339; J. Brush, 'Recent Changes in Geographical Patterns of Growth in Metropolitan Bombay and Delhi', (manuscript, Rutgers University, 1980).

22. V. Grossman, 'Multi-level planning and decision-making in Brazil with particular reference to the Northeastern region', in *Regional Disaggregation of National Policies and Plans*, ed A. Kuklinski (The Hague: Mouton, 1976); J. D. Henshell and R. P. Momsen, Jr, *A Geography of Brazilian Development* (London, 1974); A. Gilbert, *Latin American Development: A Geographical Perspective* (London: Penguin Books, 1974).

23. S. Faissol, 'Urban Growth and Economic Development in Brazil in 1960s', in *Urbanization and Counter-Urbanization*, ed Berry, pp. 169–88; W. Stöhr, 'Regional Development', *op. cit.*; B. J. L. Berry, 'The Counterurbanization Process: How General?' in *Human Settlement Systems*, ed Hansen, pp. 25–49.

24. Vining and Kontuly, 'Population Dispersal', *op. cit.;* Mera, 'Population Concentration', p. 167; B. Renaud, 'Economic Growth and Income Inequality in Korea', World Bank Staff Working Paper No. 240, Washington, 1976.

25. Sang W. Park, 'City Size Distribution in Korea', (unpublished paper, Rutgers University, 1979); Mera, 'Population Concentration', *op. cit.,* pp. 168–73.

26. Rémy Prud'homme, 'Regional Economic Policy in France', in *Public Policy and Regional Economic Development; The Experience of Nine Western Countries,* ed N. Hansen, (Cambridge, Massachusetts: Ballinger Publishing Co., 1974), pp. 33–64; Vining and Kontuly, 'Population Dispersal', *op. cit.,* and Thomas D. Bowie, *Country Labor Profile—France,* US Department of Labor, Bureau of International Affairs (Washington, DC: US Government Printing Office, 1979).

27. Vining and Kontuly, 'Population Dispersal', *op. cit.,* p. 58.

28. James L. Sundquist, *Dispersing Population: What America Can Learn from Europe* (Washington, DC: The Brookings Institute, 1975) pp. 99–144; Niles Hansen, 'French Regional Planning Experience', *Journal of the American Institute of Planners* 35 (1969): 362–8.

29. A. L. Strong, *Planned Urban Environments* (Baltimore: Johns Hopkins Press, 1971), pp. 300–1.

30. E. R. Denison and W. H. Chung, 'Economic Growth and Its Sources', in *Asia's New Giant: How the Japanese Economy Works,* ed H. Patrick and H. Rosovsky (Washington, DC: The Brookings Institute, 1976), pp. 63–151; Norman J. Glickman, 'The Japanese Urban System During a Period of Rapid Economic Development', International Institute for Applied Systems Analysis (IIASA), RM-77-25, Laxenburg, Austria, 1977; also his, 'Growth and Change in the Japanese Urban System: The Experience of the 1970s', IIASA, RM-77-39, Laxenburg, 1977; Vining and Kontuly, 'Population Dispersal', *op. cit.*

31. S. Okita, T. Kuroda, M. Yasukawa, Y. Okasaki, and K. Iio, 'Population and Development: The Japanese Experience', in *World Population and Development,* ed P. Hauser (Syracuse: Syracuse University Press, 1979), pp. 329–34; and K. Mera, *The Changing Pattern of Population Distribution in Japan and Its Implications for Developing Countries* (Tokyo: International Development Center for Japan, 1976).

32. G. Sternlieb and J. W. Hughes (eds), *Post-Industrial America: Metropolitan Decline and Inter-Regional Job Shifts* (New Brunswick, New Jersey: Center for Urban Policy Research of Rutgers University (CUPR), 1975); and their *Revitalizing the Northeast* (New Brunswick: CUPR, 1978). Such processes and shifts have been documented in publications too numerous to list here.

33. Berry, 'The Counter-urbanization Process', *op. cit.,* p. 42.

34. S. El-Shakhs, 'Development, Primacy and the Structure of Cities'.

35. Vining and Kontuly, 'Population Dispersal', *op. cit.,* p. 68.

36. The function and size of a large city may be as much a result of its position and interaction within an international (or regional) network of cities as it is the result of its position within its national system. This phenomenon has been observed in the Middle East and Latin America, and may well be the case in Western Europe. See J. Abu-Lughod, 'Problems and Policy Implications of Middle Eastern Urbanization', UNESCO, working paper, Beirut, 1971; P. O. Pedersen, *Urban Regional Development in*

Latin America: A Process of Diffusion and Integration, UNRISD Series on Regional Development, A. Kuklinski (ed), (The Hague: Mouton, 1975), p. 69.

37. Since the divergence-convergence sequence in the distribution of urban size and regional income were introduced in 1965 (El-Shakhs, 'Development, Primacy and the Structure of Cities', and Williamson, 'Regional Inequality') a large number of empirical studies of both LDCs and MDCs have generally tended to confirm such patterns (e.g. the work of McGreevey on Latin America, Mera on the Far East, Vining on Europe).

38. J. Friedman, *Urbanization, Planning and National Development* (Beverly Hills: Sage Publications, 1973); S. El-Shakhs, 'Planning for Systems of Settlements in Emerging Nations', *Town Planning Review* 47 (April 1976): 127–138.

39. The question of economies of urban size, i.e. when are large cities too large to be efficient, cannot be resolved independent of function, location, and internal organization: Richardson, 'City Size', *op. cit.,* pp. 12–15; similarly the optimality of city size distributions cannot be determined without consideration of distances, relative spatial distribution and the size of the whole system: Edwin von Boventer, 'City Size Systems: Theoretical Issues, Empirical Regularities and Planning Guides', *Urban Studies* 10 (1973): 145–162.

40. These types and their dominant charcteristics are based on a synthesis of different approaches of classification. See: El-Shakhs, 'Development, Primacy and the Structure of Cities', *op. cit.,* pp. 181–206; Pedersen, *Urban Regional Development,* pp. 92–109; and Beier *et al., The Task Ahead for Cities,* pp. 4–14.

41. W. Stöhr and H. Palme, 'Centre-Periphery Development Alternatives and their Applicability to Rural Areas in Developing Countries', paper delivered at the joint meeting of the Latin American and African Studies Associations, Houston, 1977, pp. 77–9; Pedersen, *Urban Regional Development,* W. Stöhr and F. Tödtling, 'An Evaluation of Regional Policies Experiences in Market and Mixed Economies', in *Human Settlement Systems,* ed Hansen, pp. 92–5.

42. *Ibid,* pp. 85–6; J. Wolpert, 'Behavioral Aspects of the Decision to Migrate', *Papers and Proceedings of the Regional Science Association* 15 (1965).

43. Richardson, 'City Size', *op. cit.,* p. 19.

44. Mera, 'Population Concentration', *op. cit.*

45. D. Seers, 'The New Meaning of Development', *International Development Review* 3 (1977): 2–7.

46. 'Equifinality' is a principle of general systems theory according to which the same final system state may be reached from different initial conditions and via different pathways. J. W. Hughes, *Urban Indicators, Metropolitan Evolution and Public Policy* (New Brunswick, New Jersey: CUPR 1973), p. 87.

47. Johannes F. Linn, 'Policies for Efficient and Equitable Growth of Cities in Developing Countries', World Bank Staff Working Paper No. 342, Washington, 1979; Walsh, *The Urban Challenge, op. cit.,* pp. 9–16; Beier *et al., The Task Ahead for Cities, op. cit.,* pp. 57–8; and El-Shakhs, 'The Urban Crisis', *op. cit.,* p. 582.

48. Stöhr, 'Regional Development Experience', *op. cit.,* p. 66.

49. For a detailed discussion of population distribution patterns and relationships to development, see Gosling and Lim, *Population Redistribution, op. cit.;* Hauser, *World Population and Development, op. cit.;* and the proceedings of the UNFPA Population Distribution Conference, Bangkok (1979).

50. M. P. Todaro, *Internal Migration in Developing Countries: A World Employment Study* (Geneva: International Labour Office, 1976); United Nations, Department of Economic and Social Affairs, *Trends and Characteristics of Internal Migration Since 1950* (New York: UN Demographic Studies No. 64, 1979); Sally Findley, *Planning for International Migration: A Review of Issues and Policies in Developing Countries* (Washington, DC: US Bureau of the Census, GPO 1977).

51. Richardson, 'City Size,' *op. cit.,* pp. 12–17.

52. Renaud, 'National Urbanization Policies', *op. cit.,* p. 129.

53. After decades of economic planning and planning individual cities, development regions, reclamation and resettlement projects and new towns, the government of Egypt finally turned its attention to the need for a comprehensive national urbanization policy study, which is currently underway. Egypt is by no means unique in this distinction (Brazil, Mexico, India, Nigeria and the Republic of Korea are but a few additional cases). In fact most countries still do not have national agencies with specific concerns for urbanization policies.

54. For a detailed discussion of such biases see Renaud, 'National Urbanization Policies', *op. cit.,* pp. 119–25.

55. For example, daily commuters to Cairo come from cities like Benha and Tanta as far as 100Km away, and Mexico City's urbanized area expanded from 346 to 633 sq km during the 1960s. N. A. Toulan, 'New Towns in the Greater Cairo Urban Region', (Cairo: Ministry of Development and New Communities, 1979); G. Garza and M. Schteingart, 'Mexico City: The Emerging Megalopolis', in *Metropolitan Latin America: the Challenge and the Response,* ed Cornelius and R. Kemper (Beverly Hills: Sage Publications, 1978), pp. 51–85.

56. Berry, *Urbanization and Counter-urbanization, op. cit.*

57. While employment in manufacturing has been increasing slightly in Italy and Japan, partly because of their still relatively large employment in agriculture and relatively higher rates of population growth, their service employment has been growing relatively much faster. (The United Kingdom and the Federal Republic of Germany, who witnessed absolute decline in manufacturing employment, also had the lowest rates of population growth.) See United Nations, *World Population Trends and Prospects by Country, 1950–2000: Summary Report of the 1978 Assessment* (New York: United Nations, 1979).

58. P. Haberer and F. Vonk, *Urban Revitalization* (Baltimore: Johns Hopkins Press, 1978); Sternlieb and Hughes, *Post-Industrial America, op. cit.*

59. G. V. Stephenson, 'Two Newly-Created Capitals: Islamabad and Brasilia', *Town Planning Review* 41 (July 1970).

60. Sternlieb and Hughes, *Post-Industrial America, op. cit.,* pp. 17–20.

61. Stöhr and Tödtling, 'An Evalution', *op. cit.,* p. 86.

62. Richardson, 'City Size', *op. cit.*, pp. 34–35.

63. P. Hauser, *World Population and Development, op. cit.*, p. 35; K. Griffith, *Land Concentration and Rural Poverty* (London: MacMillan, 1976).

64. D. Slater, 'Geography and Underdevelopment', *ANTIPODE* 9 (December 1977). Recently a large body of analyses in the literature have dealt with the political and socio-economic implications and problems of the growth without development processes within dependency frameworks: see, e.g., the works of S. Amin, R. Clower and G. Dalton on Africa; F. Cardoso, E. Faletto, A. Frank, A. Gilbert and C. Furtado on Latin America.

65. United Nations, *World Population Trends and Policies 1977 Monitoring Report, Vol. 77, Population Policies,* (New York: UN, 1979), Vol. II, pp. 71–7.

66. Stöhr and Tödtling, 'An Evaluation', *op. cit.*, p. 89.

67. A. R. Markusen, 'Regionalism and the Capitalist State: The Case of the United States', *Kapitalistate* 7 (Winter 1979).

68. N. Glickman, 'Financing the Japanese Urban System; Local Public Finance and Intergovernmental Relations', IIASA, RM-77-48.

69. J. L. Corragio, 'Polarization Development, and Integration', in *Regional Development and Planning,* ed A. R. Kuklinski (Leyden: Sijtoff, 1975), pp. 353–74.

70. Stöhr and Todtling, 'An Evaluation', *op. cit.,* Richardson, 'City Size', *op. cit.;* D. R. F. Taylor, 'Spatial Aspects of the Development Process', in *The Spatial Structure of Development: A Study of Kenya,* ed R. A. Obudho and D. R. F. Taylor (Boulder, Colorado: Westview Press, 1979), pp. 1–27.

71. Stöhr and Tödtling, 'An Evaluation', *op. cit.*, p. 109.

72. G. Garza and M. Schteingart, 'Mexico City', pp. 51–85; R. D. Utria, 'Some Aspects of Regional Development in Latin America', *International Social Development Review* 4 (1972): 42–56; Findley, *Planning for International Migration,* p. 101.

73. Findley, *Planning for International Migration, op. cit.,* p. 110; E. Bussey, *The Flight from Rural Poverty: How Nations Cope* (Lexington, Massachusetts: Lexington Books, 1973).

74. The term was coined by Lloyd Rodwin, in his *Nations and Cities* (Boston: Houghton-Mifflin, 1970), pp. 4–8, and covers a broad category of urban and regional decentralization strategies most frequently identified with the 'growth centre' strategy and the French experience. A large number of countries have attempted different forms of such strategies, including Argentina, Brazil, Colombia, Chile, Great Britain, India, Japan, Mexico, Nigeria, Pakistan, Peru, the Philippines, Thailand, Turkey and Venezuela. Findley, *Planning for International Migration, op. cit.,* p. 95.

75. The 'bottom-up' approach is a more recent concept which was a reaction to some of the perceived inadequacies of the hierarchical diffusion process basic to concentrated decentralization strategies: E. A. J. Johnson, *The Organization of Space in Developing Nations* (Cambridge, Massachusetts: Harvard University Press, 1970). This strategy has frequently been identified with Tanzanian and Chinese experiences; however it has been used at least in part by Israel, Mexico and Puerto Rico. S. Findley, *Planning for International Migration, op. cit.,* p. 120.

76. Richardson, 'City Size', *op. cit.,* pp. 56–7; W. Stöhr, *Regional De-*

velopment Experiences; Planning for International Migration, op. cit.; J. C. Stewart, 'Linkages and Foreign Direct Investment', *Regional Studies* 4 (1976); Glickman, 'The Japanese Urban System', *op. cit.*

77. Taylor, 'Spatial Aspects', *op. cit.;* C. Gerry, 'Petty Production and Capitalist Production in Dakar: The Crisis of the Self-Employed', *World Development* 9/10 (1978).

78. Richardson, 'City Size', *op. cit.*, p. 60.

79. Examples include growth centres and development towns in Brazil, Canada, India, Israel, United Kingdom, USA, USSR and Venezuela, among others.

80. New towns or new capital cities were developed for such objectives in Brazil, Egypt, India, Pakistan, Turkey and the United Kingdom, among others.

81. Experiences with such new towns are much more prevalent at different scales and with different degrees of success. The better-known examples are found in the metropolitan regions of London, Paris, Stockholm, Washington DC, Calcutta and Singapore.

82. Analyses of market town developments indicate positive impact on rural income and employment in Mexico, India, Morocco and Ethiopia, among others. See Findley, *Planning for International Migration, op. cit.*, p. 94.

83. J. Hardoy, 'The Planning of New Capital Cities', in *Planning of Metropolitan Areas and New Towns* (New York: United Nations, 1969), pp. 232–49.

84. For instance the shift of the capital from Calcutta or (for a few years) from Tripoli did not significantly affect their growth. In Cameroon, despite the removal of governmental functions to an inland city, the major port city of Douala is still growing too fast; a similar situation may occur in Nigeria.

85. Findley, *Planning for International Migration, op. cit.*, pp. 75–91.

86. S. Migot-Adholla, 'Rural Development Policy and Equality', in *Politics and Public Policy in Kenya and Tanzania*, ed J. D. Brakan and J. J. Okumu (New York: Praeger, 1979), pp. 165–72.

87. A. Berler, *New Towns in Israel* (Jerusalem: University Press, 1970).

88. Stöhr and Palme, 'Centre-Periphery Development Alternatives', *op. cit.*

89. Several western European nations had parallel experiences in urban renewal/community development in central cities (e.g. Paris, Brussels, Milan). For adaptive reuse see R. Burchell and D. Listokin, *The Adaptive Reuse Handbook* (New Brunswick, New Jersey: Rutgers CUPR, 1980); Haberer and Vonk, *Urban Revitalization, op. cit.*

90. Strong, *Planned Urban Environments, op. cit.*, pp. 37–43 and 363–73.

91. Abu-Lughod, 'The Urban Future', *op. cit.*, p. 1.

92. Stöhr, 'Regional Development Experiences', *op. cit.*

93. It has been suggested that such improvement for women can include the introduction of household and small-scale enterprises, child and youth care and recreation facilities, prepared food marketing, inexpensive transport to work locations, handicrafts, access to informal education and mass media outlets, and health care and nutrition centres: Vincent and Pauline Milone, 'Planning for Poor Urban Women in Third World Communities: Project Design for Fertility Reduction and Income Generation', (unpublished paper, 1980), p. 7.

94. Johnson, *The Organization of Space, op. cit.*, p. 419.

SALAH EL-SHAKHS

95. Several countries have designed integrated rural development programmes explicitly to slow rural-to-urban migration. These include India,
Thailand, the Philippines, Israel, Pakistan, Colombia, Kenya, Mexico and
the United Republic of Tanzania. See Findley, *Planning for International
Migration, op. cit.*, p. 114.
96. N. Hansen, 'Growth Strategies and Human Settlement Systems in
Developing Countries', IIASA RM-76-2, Laxenburg, Austria, January 1976,
p. 12.
97. J. Friedman and M. Douglas, *Agropolitan Development: Towards a
New Strategy for Regional Planning in Asia* (Nagoya, Japan: UNCRD,
1975).
98. Stöhr and Palme, 'Centre Periphery Development Alternatives', *op.
cit.*, pp. 28–32.
99. In fact they tend to have more characteristics in common than they
do with smaller urban centres in their own national systems. Huges, *Urban
Indicators, op. cit.*

Sources

Tables 5.1, 5.3, 5.4, 5.5, 5.6, 5.7, 5.9, 5.13 and 5.14 are based on: Kingsley
Davis, *World Urbanization, 1950–1970, Vol. 1: Basic Data for Cities, Countries and Regions,* Population Monograph Series, No. 4 (Berkeley: Institute
of International Studies, University of California, 1969, revised edition),
Table A; Bertrand Renaud, 'National Urbanization Policies in Developing
Countries', World Bank Staff Working Paper No. 347, Washington, DC,
1976, pp. 144, 189; Shail, Jain, 'Size Distribution of Income: A Compilation
of Data', World Bank, Washington, DC, 1975; United Nations, Department
of Economic and Social Affairs, Population Division, 'Trends and Prospects
in Urban and Rural Population, 1980–2000, As Assessed in 1973–74', (E
SA/P/WP 54) 25 April 1975, Table A; and United Nations Conference on
Trade and Development, *Handbook of International Trade and Development Statistics, 1979* (New York: United Nations, 1979), Table 6.1A.

Other sources are credited on the appropriate tables.

Rome Declaration on Population and the Urban Future

ISSUED BY THE INTERNATIONAL CONFERENCE
ON POPULATION AND THE URBAN FUTURE

The International Conference on Population and the Urban Future, sponsored by the United Nations Fund for Population Activities (UNFPA), took place in Rome, Italy, from 1 to 4 September 1980. The conference was attended by mayors, administrators and planners from 41 cities whose populations are projected to be 5 million or more by the year 2000, as well as by national planners from the 31 countries where these cities are located. This Declaration was issued at the conclusion of the conference.

Preamble

1. We, the participants of the International Conference on Population and the Urban Future
—having assembled in Rome from September 1 through September 4, 1980 at the invitation of the United Nations Fund for Population Activities (UNFPA)
—grateful for the warm and generous hospitality extended to us by the City of Rome and Government of Italy
—having considered the present conditions and future trends of population growth and the problems generated by rapid urbanization in various parts of the world

hereby issue this declaration:

2. We believe that the objectives and the measures set out in this declaration will contribute towards the achievement of the

goals of the World Population Plan of Action, the Colombo Declaration on Population and Development, the New International Economic Order, the recommendations of the Vancouver Conference on Human Settlements, the Action Plan of the Stockholm Conference on the Human Environment, and of other international strategies for improving the living conditions of people all over the world.

The Need

3. It is estimated that around the year 1800 less than 3 per cent of the population of the world lived in urban areas. By 1920, the figure had risen to fourteen per cent. By 1950, urban populations formed a quarter of total world population. By the end of the century, over half of the world's population will be urban. In the next two decades, the world will undergo, as a result of the urbanization process, the most radical changes ever in social, economic and political life.

4. The impact of urbanization will differ in the different regions of the world. In 1980 the total world population is estimated at 4.4 billion and is projected to increase to 6.2 billion by the year 2000. Urban population will increase from 1.8 billion to 3.2 billion during the same period. Over two billion of this total urban population will be in the developing countries. Today, the number of cities with populations of 5 million or more is 26 with a combined population of 252 million. It is projected that by the year 2000, there will be 60 such cities with a population of 650 million. Approximately 45 of these "supercities" will be in the developing world.

5. We recognize that, historically, the city has been the engine of development and the forge of human creative energies. In fact, the city has often been the place in which civilization has blossomed. We believe that the process of urbanization can be harnessed to achieve mankind's goal of just, peaceful and lasting progress. But if this is to happen, urbanization must take place under planned and orderly conditions.

6. Today, as we review the situation around the world, we find that these planned and orderly conditions for urbanization for the

most part do not exist. We find that the problems confronting urban settlements are in fact already acute in many parts of the world. They include shortages in virtually every service, amenity and support required for tolerable urban living. Housing and shelter, basic health services, sanitation, clean air and potable water, education, transport, energy supplies, open spaces and recreational facilities—all these are lacking in many parts of the world. Moreover, under conditions of unplanned urbanization, the situation is becoming worse rather than better.

7. Economic problems—such as unemployment, underemployment, lack of means of livelihood, poverty and deprivation—loom large. Social problems—crime, delinquency, social segregation and the exploitation of certain groups, e.g., migrants and urban squatters—are becoming increasingly acute, as are environmental problems such as congestion and pollution. These questions are not confined to the developing countries. In the more developed countries, the inability of cities to cope with the problems which they face has become one of the dominant characteristics of the late 20th century.

8. Unplanned urbanization may generate tension between groups and classes within the city itself; it may also generate tension between urban and rural areas within national boundaries. Peace itself, which is the precondition for development, may be put in jeopardy. For, as the Colombo Declaration on Population and Development stated, one of the principal threats to peace is the social unrest caused by the accumulation of human fear and hopelessness. Fear and hopelessness can accumulate both quickly and enduringly in the hearts of the urban poor when their aspirations are not realized.

9. We believe that the pace and pattern of urbanization, and the nature of the social and economic development that takes place, are crucially influenced by demographic trends. In the less developed countries, migration from rural areas formerly contributed the major part of urban growth. Now, natural increase—the excess of births over deaths—generally contributes 60 per cent of urban growth. In the more developed countries, 60 per cent of urban growth is accounted for by migration. We believe that the process of urbanization can only be managed where the demographic factors contributing to this process are themselves

managed through economic, social, political and cultural measures. We must seek to match population with resources in cities, in regions, in countries and—ultimately—in the world itself.

Objectives

10. To improve and enrich the quality of life for these increasing numbers of urban dwellers—all of them individuals needing food, shelter, clean water, work, education and medical care, as well as a decent physical and social environment to live in—and to avoid a continued aggravation of the urban situation over the next decades, a fairer distribution of wealth between nations is necessary. At the same time internal changes are necessary to ensure an equitable distribution of resources and a fair and just society within each nation. The objective of managed population growth and planned urbanization must be to achieve a balanced allocation of resources and development opportunities and of the economic and social benefits resulting from them.

Recommendations

11. In order to achieve these objectives, it is vital that countries develop a strategy for national planning for the urban future. Such strategies, supported by appropriate legislation and funding should include, among others, three important elements, namely:
1) the formulation of comprehensive national population policies
2) policies for balanced development, and
3) policies for improvement of urban areas.
12. *The formulation of comprehensive national population policies.* All countries which do not yet have comprehensive population policies and programmes should formulate them. A comprehensive national population policy should, among other things, specify national and sub-national goals on the rate of growth of population, on levels of fertility and mortality and on the distribution of population between urban and rural areas. It

– 184

will need to be fully integrated into the process of development planning, particular emphasis being given to health, education, housing, nutrition, employment and environmental conditions. We urge that such policies be formulated in all countries by 1985.

13. *Policies for balanced development.* Plans for the redistribution of population, as part of a comprehensive national population policy, will only succeed if they form part of a strategy for balanced development. Such a strategy should be aimed at encouraging a balanced pattern of urban setlements, i.e. small, intermediate and large cities, and at the economic development of rural areas. The elimination of glaring inequalities and disparities in the quality of life and opportunity between urban and rural areas should reduce the flow of migration from the countryside to the cities. Similarly, the provision of better information to rural populations about economic opportunities and social amenities—or the lack of them—available in the cities should permit potential migrants to have a clearer vision of the future that awaits them.

14. *Policies for the improvement of urban areas.* The shanty towns and slum areas of the cities are mainly populated by migrants from the rural areas and the urban poor. Most of the urban services, such as educational and health facilities, potable water and urban sanitation are beyond the reach of these people. It is important that cities pay special attention to problems of these vulnerable groups, and that the sub-cultures of such groups be studied. The object should be to identify the values and dynamics of vulnerable groups. Special programmes should be developed aimed at facilitating the adaptation and integration into urban living of disadvantaged population groups such as new migrants, poor families, children and youth, the homeless and elderly. Such programmes should also be aimed at transmitting suitable skills to improve job opportunities.

15. The economic opportunities, in the context of national, regional and local development policies, offered by judicious 'upgrading' of shanty towns and other marginal settlements should be recognized and exploited wherever possible. Policies and programmes should be developed to recognize and strengthen the role of the transitional or informal sector in the economy.

16. High land value is often one of the principal limits to the

185 –

implementation of urban plans. Therefore, rules and regulations should be enacted to control the real estate market in order to avoid an unbalanced land use and to let local administrations carry out a fair urban planning for the different social groups.

17. More generally, it is necessary to achieve a revitalization of the cities as centres of intense social activity and communication, culture, heritage and civilization.

18. Some measures are common to all three aspects of the above strategy. They will need to be adopted as appropriate at the national, regional, metropolitan and local levels. The most important are:

a) Creation or strengthening of the necessary institutions needed to formulate and implement policies for integrating and coordinating urban development within the process of economic, social and physical development itself.

b) Improvement of collection of population and related data required for policies and programmes for development and integration of urban planning in accordance with national objectives, and promotion of related research.

c) Encouraging the full participation of the population at large and their community organizations in the urban development process both at the planning and the implementation stage of policy and programme development.

d) Establishing or strengthening measures to enable all couples and individuals to have the basic right to decide freely and responsibly the number and spacing of their children and to have the information, education and means to do so.

e) Building up of an institutional framework for exchange of experience, views and ideas on population and urban development between planners, policy makers and administrators within and between countries. This should permit the effective monitoring of urbanization trends and of the implementation of the policies and measures suggested above.

Commitment to Action

19. The measures proposed in this Declaration require action primarily at the national, regional, metropolitan or local levels.

International cooperation and assistance is, however, urgently needed if these measures are to be successfully carried out. The various international bodies concerned, including non-governmental organizations, are called upon to take the necessary steps within their mandates to help cities and nations to deal effectively with present and future urbanization problems. Governments of developed countries and others able to contribute to international assistance should intensify their support, both in bilateral assistance programmes and through contributions to multilateral agencies, for the activities in the field of population and urbanization covered by this Declaration. In this connection, we welcome the initiative of the United Nations Fund for Population Activities in convening this Conference and urge governments to increase their support of UNFPA so that it may, within the framework of its mandate, devote increasing attention to the problems of urbanization, including monitoring the implementation of this Declaration in collaboration with United Nations and other international bodies.

20. Finally, we dedicate ourselves to devote our best endeavors towards the attainment of the objectives and recommendations of the Declaration, consistent with other national priorities and development goals. We believe that the present decade, the decade of the 1980s, is the time for intensive effort and for the necessary re-orientation of the response of peoples and governments to the urbanization problem. In the past the development of the city and of urban living has greatly expanded mankind's horizons. It has permitted the enrichment of life, as exemplified by the contributions of science, the arts and education; by tremendously expanded options for goods and services; and by the provision of a better level of living for all. We ask no less for the future.

307.76
H 376

66082